The Stuff of Life

ALSO AVAILABLE FROM BLOOMSBURY

Spacecraft, Timothy Morton
Surplus-Enjoyment: A Guide For The Non-Perplexed, Slavoj Žižek
Prophetic Culture: Recreation For Adolescents, Federico Campagna

The Stuff of Life

Timothy Morton

BLOOMSBURY ACADEMIC
LONDON • NEW YORK • OXFORD • NEW DELHI • SYDNEY

BLOOMSBURY ACADEMIC
Bloomsbury Publishing Plc
50 Bedford Square, London, WC1B 3DP, UK
1385 Broadway, New York, NY 10018, USA
29 Earlsfort Terrace, Dublin 2, Ireland

BLOOMSBURY, BLOOMSBURY ACADEMIC and the Diana logo are
trademarks of Bloomsbury Publishing Plc

First published in Great Britain 2023

For legal purposes the Acknowledgements on p. ix constitute an extension
of this copyright page.

Cover design by Ben Anslow
Cowboy hat (© MyPro / Shutterstock);Lip gloss (© Marina Akinina / Getty Images);
Hen (© FORGEM / iStock);Lizard (© MurzillA / Shutterstock);
Tablets (© Hasyim Asngari / Dreamstime)

A catalogue record for this book is available from the British Library.

A catalog record for this book is available from the Library of Congress.

ISBN: HB: 978-1-3502-4047-6
        PB: 978-1-3502-4048-3
        ePDF: 978-1-3502-4049-0
        eBook: 978-1-3502-4050-6

Typeset by RefineCatch Limited, Bungay, Suffolk
Printed and bound in Great Britain

To find out more about our authors and books visit www.bloomsbury.com
and sign up for our newsletters.

For Claire and Simon
the stuff of life indeed

Contents

Acknowledgments

Thanks so very, very much to Liza Thompson, who believed in this project, and then some. And thank you Federico Campagna, who inspired me to write it, about four years ago. It was an extraordinary intuition. I'm still not sure how he had it. It's been life changing. It's changed how I think and write. This book has been slowly coming together since then, thanks to Federico and Liza who saw what it could be, before I did. Writing it was a dream and a treat. And thank you Myshel Prasad. I don't know how to, not all of it. There's so much. I don't know. Thank you Si Leong for the demonic angels and the angelic demons. Thank you Jeffrey Kripal for blowing my mind since 2011. And thank you to my research assistants, Taylin Nelson, Anne Rubsamen and V. Lundquist. Your help was invaluable.

The epigraph is from in *The Complete Poetry and Prose of William Blake*, ed. David V. Erdman (New York: Doubleday, 1988).

There is a Grain of Sand in Lambeth that Satan cannot find
Nor can his Watch Fiends find it: tis translucent & has many
Angles
But he who finds it will find Oothoons palace, for within
Opening into Beulah every angle is a lovely heaven
But should the Watch Fiends find it, they would call it Sin.

WILLIAM BLAKE

0

Roses

Life flows on, whether you like it or not, within you and without you.

"And life flows on within you and without you." The stark, beautiful, psychedelic truth, cold and shivering with sitars and tablas: it's George Harrison's song that opens side two of *Sergeant Pepper's Lonely Hearts Club Band*. Enough of the whimsy of "Being for the Benefit of Mister Kite." Time to stop posing. Time to start talking about things. About *things*.

The Stuff of Life is an ambiguous phrase. It could mean "what makes life worth living"—in this phrase, "stuff" has a nourishing texture, a depth. Or it could mean "the stuff you don't notice, that makes up your life"—in this version, "stuff" doesn't have *enough* of a texture, it's vague and ambient. It could mean "stuff happens, tough luck"—like that t-shirt from the 1990s that said "shit happens." It could mean "the ingredients of biological life." The stuff that happens whether you mean it to or not. Within you. Without you.

Life is about all kinds of ambiguity: ambiguous feelings, ambiguous situations. Ambiguity doesn't mean vagueness.

Ambiguity means accuracy. If you've been to the eye doctor, you'll know that it always comes down to a choice between two solutions. The technician is going, "Is it number one, or number two? Number one, or number two?" At first it's easy: you can choose number one because number two just doesn't work as well. But eventually, you get down to a choice between two solutions that are almost perfect but not quite. They can't be perfect because you don't have infinite money and lenses can't be infinitely ground and doctors can't be infinitely good and optometry can't be infinitely perfect. You have an ambiguous choice. *Ambo* is Latin for "on both sides." Ambiguity means you have a choice between two or more very precise options. You have a dilemma. But that's actually great. If you can't tell between two equally not-quite-perfect lenses for your new glasses, it means that whichever you choose, *you will have an accurate prescription*.

Ambiguity is a signal of accuracy. Life is ambiguous like that. Survival can't be. Survival is a one-size-fits-all lens you buy in the supermarket because there's no time for subtleties. You just have to read the sign so you can get the train so you can get the fuck out of there.

For me, "life" is very different from "survival." I've been surviving for ages, and I only just started to feel like I was alive. Even that phrase, "like I was alive," is ambiguous—it might mean I'm an android, or I'm dreaming. It does feel like that, most days. "Survival" is very sure of itself. "Survive" means "definitely don't die, no matter what." In survival mode, life and death are opposites. Being alive . . . I'm not so sure it's the opposite of death.

"Alive" is a needle quivering between zero and infinity. At zero, there's just ceasing to exist at all. What happens when you "fade away" or rot into the soil or quietly implode. At infinity, there's endless repetition: the roiling, churning machinery. This is what Neil Young called "burning out"—he said "I'd rather burn out than fade away," to which John Lennon replied, "You gotta be joking, I'd fade away any day." And look what happened to him. This end, the ceaseless, exhausting repetition, is what Sigmund Freud called the *death drive*, and our lives—I really do mean *our* (it's worldwide and it's about all of us now, and by *all of us* I mean *all life on this planet*)—is so far over to the burnout. From the point of view of survival mode, being alive looks like letting yourself die. That needle is a long way towards the other end. It's quivering in the middle. It's ambiguous. The needle has accepted death. It's scary. Don't go there. "Just keep swimming, just keep swimming," goes the mantra of Dory, the obsessive fish in the film *Finding Nemo*.

Forgive me if you know this already. You probably do. I only just figured this out two years ago, when I had my first break from work in twenty years. I was scared to take a sabbatical of six months from my university job. What would happen to me if I stopped? Stopped to smell the roses, as they say? Would the smell be so intoxicating—so hypnotic, so beautiful—that I might forget to survive?

The answer to those questions is yes. I stopped to smell the roses. And this book started to happen.

The Stuff of Life is a memoir about the things in my life. Things like BBC children's TV programs from the 1970s. Things like a stick of concealer. Things to which we give the word "thing" as opposed to "person." It's a philosophy memoir. So as we stop to smell the roses, we will also be pausing to reflect.

Jacques Derrida's best advice to his students was, *decelerate*.

This book is about "stuff" for a deep reason. This book is about a principle of "flat ontology" that belongs to something called *object-oriented ontology*. Object-oriented ontology or OOO is how I like to see the world. "Ontology" means the study of how things exist. Science tells you *what* exists. Ontology tells you *how*. And how is that, for an object-oriented thinker? To be a stick is to be just as real as the dog chasing the stick, just as real as the human who threw the stick for the dog to fetch.

"Flat" doesn't mean "just as important"—you have to decide for yourself and with others, if you hold this view called OOO, what counts as important. Whose sides are you on? Flat means that things exist in the same way as one another. If a candlestick exists, it exists in the same way as the idea of a candlestick, or a sentence about a candlestick, or the memory of a candlestick. They all exist in the same way: you can't grasp them. Nothing can totally grasp them.

To be is to be mysterious.

OOO is about things that you can't quite see. It's as if things have their own underworld. A black hole has an obvious underworld, because light won't escape from it. But so does my black and white cat, Oliver. So does my life, considered as a thing. I can't survey the whole thing all at once—when I do, I lose details. When I focus on a detail, I lose the whole thing. You can't find the underworld of a thing anywhere, because it's everywhere.

OOO reveals a world peppered with underworlds, like an icescape full of crevasses. This is a perfectly normal scientific attitude. The more we know about things—the more data we have—the stranger they become. Data just means "things that are given" in Latin. The data science collects have to do with measurements such as velocity and temperature and frequency. But other things are given to us—the smell of a rose, the prick of a thorn, an annoying realization that I don't have a bandage on me. Whenever you try to look for the underworld, you find more data. You find ghosts, like Odysseus when he talks to the shades in the underworld. Ghosts of things.

I like to bring in a banana when I illustrate this in a lecture. So you've got this banana. You give it a lick—you have a banana lick. You draw the banana. You have a banana drawing. You measure the banana. You have banana measurements. You remember all the times you ate a banana. You have banana memories. You slice open the banana, hoping to find the real banana-nature inside. You have a banana slice. You bite a chunk off the banana—you have a banana bite.

What you don't have is the *banana banana*. You have bites, slices, measurements, memories, drawings, licks. I'm saying *banana banana* to name the banana in itself, the *banane an sich*. Now imagine the banana becomes sentient, develops a consciousness, and goes on a chat show. "So, tell me about yourself." "I'm bananas" (audience laughs). "You have a multiple personality disorder?" (laughter). These are banana sayings. The sayings get collected in a book, called *What Bananas Are Saying about Themselves*. It's a banana book. The banana gives up somewhere deep inside, and seeks out a therapist to help with its existential angst—maybe a cucumber, the banana has heard they're cool. While lying on the couch the banana opens up: "I first realized there was a problem when I found myself being talked about by this philosopher—it was so traumatic and now I get triggered whenever I see the word *philosophy*."

That's banana therapy speech. That's not the banana either. Even the banana can't access the banana banana! Even if the measurements are 100% exact, the measurements are not the banana. A few months from now, there will be a whole different set of measurements, as the banana liquefies in a landfill. Those measurements won't be the banana either. A biologist puts wafer thin slices of banana onto a slide and examines them under a microscope, as powerful as you like. She is collecting data about banana cells. That's not the banana banana either. The banana was once attached to a banana tree, but that tree has its own problems with accessing itself, I'm afraid. So you won't find the banana banana there, either. You won't find it at the moment when the banana flower is transmuting into the banana fruit. You won't find it in the banana's DNA—that's banana DNA.

Bananas have underworlds.

We also know that when you rewind the tape called *evolution*, you might not even end up with a banana if you played the tape forwards again. Genetic mutation is random. Genuinely new things can happen. Bananas are contingent, miraculous, mysterious things saturated with time, their own sweet time as a matter of fact. They're yellow and delicious and soft and good to use as examples—and they have an absolutely unspeakable shadow side, a side that isn't even a side, so you can't even say that about it. The banana is nowhere to be found other than in the banana data. A banana is not an apple. And yet banana data is not a banana!

This brings us to the fact of you as a "thing," as an OOO being with an underworld. This book calls such a thing a *soul*. Soul is a beautiful short word for something true. Let go of the prejudice that *soul* means some kind of smoke or liquid in a bottle—the normal, oppressive, mind–body dualism popular in medieval patriarchal thought, which far too many of us are busy retweeting.

If you drop the idea that *soul* is some kind of substance, some more-real-than-this-world continuity of underlying stuff, you are taking the next important step in reclaiming this word. Soul: everything you ever did, everything you touched, all the conversations you had, all your thoughts and feelings, the tree you sat under reading Henry James when you were seventeen, the strange chair that gave you whiplash just by sitting in it, that room in that divey apartment in New York . . . All that is a galaxy of things that doesn't have an obvious center or an obvious edge. But still it's you, it's not your Uncle David. It's not your tuxedo cat. It's "you," but it isn't. It's not bounded and solid. Why do we always think "object" means something bounded and solid and hard?

This is a memoir in which I sample this soul, which I dare not even call "mine." It's more like I belong to it. I turn down the volume on the other sentient beings in my life, and turn up the volume on arc lights, packets of noodles and cowboy costumes. These are the things that you might think are tangential to life as a human being. They're just props, or furniture . . . the stage set for your ego. They're "stuff" in that vague sense I was sketching just now. But there you are, among them. And how you ignore them is also how they affect you. There's no escape. And you're not on stage. You're not performing to get approval from a teacher or a god or the internet, some grizzled old narcissist with a gray beard who works in heaven or college or intimidates people with his truck, someone who mostly wants to hurt you unless you impress him, you may have to burn the whole thing down to get the A . . . Well you are performing like that, but that's the problem. Because all the other beings on the planet are not your props, and the transcendental *New York Times* theater critic is never going to be arriving. This fact is becoming more and more frighteningly clear as the climate emergency heats up.

The things in *The Stuff of Life* aren't necessarily physical objects. Ideas, memories, even grief are things. The first chapter is about afterimages—a particular one that I used to call an *electric peanut*. I used to play the game "electric peanuts" with my cousins every Saturday when I was about eleven years old. I would switch on a powerful lamp in a darkened room. We all stared at it for a minute, then when I switched off the lamp, we would see the peanut-shaped, rainbow-colored afterimages. This leads to a discussion of the way new ways of being and new ideas can emerge, a dialectic between ideology and what Raymond Williams calls *the structure of feeling*.

Lest you think that this is of no political significance, Fredric Jameson, for one, has spoken of the political power of the ability to visualize, from which comes all art but also all of our powers to imagine the future, a time different from this one, assuming we wish things to be different (which I do, very much). And lest you think this isn't really a "thing," there's a century of phenomenology backing up the idea that my electric peanuts, like logical propositions and thoughts in general, are mind-independent entities in their own right. They had better be, otherwise as symptoms of brains we would be lost in a world where all news was fake news.

Philosopher certainly doesn't mean "someone (preferably male) who has big ideas." Literally, philosophy means *the love of wisdom*. The *philos* part means love; the *sophy* part means wisdom. Those two things are feelings. If you had to choose between "Wisdom is a set of ideas or instructions" and "Wisdom is a feeling," I'm pretty sure you would go with "Wisdom is a feeling."

Some think philosophy is about having big ideas and then competing about who has the biggest idea. This isn't correct. Philosophy is the love of wisdom, or wisdom in love. Philosophy is like a car driving down a street. The ideas are like the lampposts you pass on your way. They just come up, around you, one by one. But you shouldn't concentrate on them so hard. If you do you might hit a lamppost. That's not a great way to drive.

Having an idea often means thinking you can see something. In English we say "I see!" when we think we have an idea. This idea of seeing something is not in the word *philosophy*. When you love something you can't see it very well. You don't know exactly why you love this person. If you did, it might mean that the relationship is over! There is always a mystery part of being in love. Love has to do with time, like grief. Seeing an idea has to do with something you think is outside time—it appears in some way always true.

One "object" I talk about is *grief*. Now there's a thing that you just can't fit into a neat little box. You can't have ideas about grief. That's because it has a very special quality. You can't get on top of it. You just can't. Grief is all the stuff you just can't get on top of. I take grief to be our inevitably painful past (we are made out of traumas) yearning to give our present a massage. It's the kind of massage that results in doubling over with the urge to vomit, and that ends in deep physical as well as psychic sensations of well-being. This "inner bodyworker" called grief is never given a chance in Western culture, and it should, lest we repeat or reinforce the past—of slavery, for example—in the attempt to ignore how the bodyworker wants to hold us and smooth us out.

One of my objects is a London Underground train and how it showed me, who grew up on bare floorboards, that there could be a future, as scary as its industrial roaring and terrifying loneliness on the daily 7am journey to school could be.

Another is a stick of concealer, a more recent object that I relate to as a person who has recently discovered something very important about themselves as a being—something whose presence cast confused and confusing and very painful shadows all my life. I am a non-binary gender person.

Nowhere besides those vital and fraught areas of gender and race do you get to see so obviously how data is not the same as things, and how facts are interpretations of data. Consider an incident from 1992, which I now realize is about thirty years ago. I had grown my hair long for several years, while I was doing my

Ph.D. My girlfriend at the time had long hair too, but it was my long hair plus my face or my eyes or how I held my body that led to that incident in the restaurant. The staff saw me as a girl. They kicked us out for kissing. "We don't serve your kind in here."

It took us ten minutes to figure out what had happened. I remember the surge of pride. I remember marching into the Dean's office saying "I have objective evidence that the restaurant around the corner is homophobic." I was sure the Dean would listen. She did. Princeton had harsh words with that restaurant that week.

It seems natural now that I was so happy I "was" a girl. That's the curious thing about "objects." They're never what you think they are. I'm talking of my own body now, my being, not just my arms and legs. But this feminine aspect of it was hiding for ages—in plain sight. Other people knew me better than I knew myself, which is neurologically *and* phenomenologically totally predictable. My way of accessing myself created this fact that I was male. A fact is always an interpretation of data. That's not some kind of postmodern "relativist" thing to say. That's modern science. I had interpreted the Tim data to mean "Tim is a man," and this had been verified by peer review. Authorities such as parents and school bullies had insisted on it, in ways that were benevolent and not-so benevolent. How was I to know? I fancied girls, therefore . . . Fancying girls is data. You don't have to be a man to fancy girls—as I write that the gigantic "DUH" in my head insists on being typed.

Your body withdraws, just like bananas. Body hugging black tops withdraw. Long hair withdraws. So does your face. There's a certain "adult male" look, a way of holding your face. I can't describe it. I used to think it was a "grownup" or "serious" face but now I see it as a masculinity performance, and masculinity very often performs "grownup" and "serious." I've never done this face. I look at photos of my schoolmates. I look at those photos and go "Wow, what am I?" I can't do that face. I've never tried to do that face. I don't want to do that face. Sorry, ninety percent of the guys I see—I hate that face. I hate it worse than that incredible strong grip handshake jerk thing that people do. The one that says "You can rely on me next time we're on a yacht together, and I'm totally not a creep." Those handshake people very often overlap with the man face people.

All that data, all those performances—it's all just data. I know. I know it in my bones. I know more than having doted on OOO for ten years. I loved OOO for that immediately because it made me smile. I know deep down that masculinity is a performance and that gender is a construct. I know in my feelings and my encounters with people in restaurants and with slack-jawed shop assistants in High Street Kensington.

Now I feel relaxed about it because I was shown my blind spot. Mostly you *are* a kind of blind spot in your own field of vision, like the cursor blinking in front of all the words on the screen. You're the best example you know of how objects "withdraw" from access. What's missing from every landscape painting? The person "in" the painting who's looking at it, not just the painter, but you, looking at it, being taken in by the perspective because you're standing the right way in front of it. A landscape painting is a sort of inverted selfie. What's missing from every selfie? Actual you. However many baby pictures you upload to Facebook (I don't like this habit), no one will see the actual baby there. Maybe that's the real reason you do it. Not to show off your baby, not to make them visible, but as the perfect octopus ink—mountains of baby data, to conceal the actual baby.

1

Electric Peanuts

"C'mon everyone. I want to show you a thing called *Electric Peanuts*."

I am at my grandfather's house. My mum's father. His wife Ruth has died. He is living in a simple ground-floor flat with a lovely garden, about ten minutes' march from my mum's maisonette at the bottom of Arthur Road, Wimbledon Park, near the tennis, London, England, Europe (at the time. . .). Grandfather, "Grampy," was now a handyman, *No Job too Small* was his slogan in the local paper, the *Wimbledon Guardian*. He had been a patent barrister. He had always been a socialist and a Marxist. He hadn't gone on the boat to the front with the officers, when he was sent to north Africa during World War II. He went with the privates, out of solidarity. The officers' boat was sunk by a U-Boat. You're reading this because my grandfather was a communist.

It's 1978. I love aliens. I think aliens were trying to contact me. I had seen *Close Encounters of the Third Kind*. I want very, very much to meet an alien.

I feel like an alien.

An idea popped in my head that aliens and alienation are expressions of human superpowers. It was 2018.

I didn't know how much I had survived. That's how much I had survived.

My cousin Lindsay, two years younger than me—I am ten, she is eight. My other cousins Debbie and Katie, daughters of Uncle David. Yet more cousins, Lexi, Vikki and Arli (Charlotte). Lexi and Vikki are older than me. Lexi is the oldest. Lexi is in the living room with the grownups. When you got to about thirteen you graduated to be in that room and were offered little sips of vermouth and talked about grown up things. Me and the younger cousins watch *Doctor Who* and then adjourn to the front room where we eat Mr Kipling's petit fours. I like the yellow one and the pink one.

It's 2000. I'm reading *Being and Nothingness* for the third time. I'm house-sitting for some professors at the University of Pennsylvania. Jean-Paul Sartre intimidates me. Jean-Paul Sartre has a thing about pink cakes. The pink is totally cake, or the cake is totally pink. You're eating pink. You don't see purple or pink. You see a purple flower, a pink cake. If you're imagining a "pure color" right now you're actually imagining a blob of some kind— it's a funny shape, but it's still a shape. A thing.

I turn off all the lights and draw the curtains.

"Now everyone, stare at this lamp." I switch on the lamp. It's a functional, grandfatherly lamp.

"Stare really hard, keep staring ... now!" Everyone stared at the bulb, especially Lindsay. It was probably a sixty-watt one from the hardware shop in town that Grampy liked to go to. I associated him with the smell of wood shavings. Suddenly, I switched off the light.

My mum had no money, and Electric Peanuts was a free light show, and it made me think of aliens. Alien phantasms, hovering in space, defying gravity. Everyone could see them.

Electric peanuts. All the colors of the rainbow, peanut-sized and peanut-shell shaped. Now I think about it, they were shaped like Hindu and Buddhist vajras: stylized thunderbolts, or diamonds, or both. When Indra throws a vajra it returns directly to his hand. *Vajra mind* is an electric peanut, the electric peanut part of your mind. The part that they can't touch. Them, the thoughts, the abusers, the snotty kids at my new school, a private one. Everyone else had a car. I had bare floorboards and electric peanuts.

What the fuck are they, these electric peanuts? They're made by your eyes and by an electric light bulb. They happen within you, and they happen without you. *What are they?* What a thing is, it's always receding, like the future. In a way it is the future. When OOO says that things withdraw, it means they have a future, they have an underworld. Like with a mirage, you're always the same distance from this future—an infinite one. That doesn't mean it's far, far away if you measure it with a tape measure. It means it's uncountably "there." You have no idea how close or how far. It's like when you look at the pyramids in the inserts of Pink Floyd's *The Dark Side of the Moon.* Are they two meters away, two miles, two light years? The distance is just . . . distance, without a number. It's what Immanuel Kant calls the sublime. The feel of "on," that sound your computer makes when you start it up, no matter what comes up on the screen a few seconds later.

Those electric peanuts hanging there in space, somehow, before your eyes, in your eyes, in your optic nerve . . . where are they? They're just there, the there-ness defying anything to do with tape measures. That's what we call *withdrawal* in OOO. You can't say, you can speak . . . it's there but you can't speak it, locate it, pin it down. It's the future. Look at your watch or a clock and try to point to the future. Where exactly is it, on the clock? How many nanometers away from the current time of 3:04pm? It's not different, it's not the same. What is an electric peanut?

The unspeakable withdrawal of futurality is accompanied by a symptom—you can't see it. You can only see the stuff that isn't that. So everywhere you look, the future isn't. But what does that even mean? What will the last word of this sentence be, black hole, elephant, stock taking, loss, banana?

An afterimage. It's your body. Your body isn't a binary machine with on and off and nothing else. An afterimage shows you how it oozes with time. There are flows, lags. Impressions. Influences. That word means *things flowing in, inflows, flowings-in*. Influenza, the Italian. The world infects us, wonderfully, horribly, unconsciously, indifferently.

One thing an electric peanut is: *innocent*. It never did any harm. *Innocent* doesn't mean *ignorant*. It means *not-harming*. An electric peanut is the total innocence of the aesthetic dimension, just the appearing-ness of things.

But we love to talk in absolutes and in binaries: intellectuals, most of all. Intellect folds the laundry of the world. But the world isn't like that. Think about the idea that "everything is a lie," or "everything is ideology." But if everything really is ideology, then so is that sentence, and you might be deceived. So everything can't be ideology. It's like saying everything is a lie. For that to be true, one thing can't be a lie—that sentence. So *true* and *false* must be different.

Intellect isn't all that. Intelligence is a feeling really, a feel. The feel of intellect-ing. Intellect is just how you fold the laundry. Intelligence is how your t-shirt feels against your skin.

But *true* and *false* are not that different. They overlap. Maybe there's a necessary illusory quality to things that you just can't shake. If you try to shake it, you get patriarchy and you pathologize people who hallucinate, even though anyone with a functioning visual system can see an electric peanut, it's a communist aesthetic of the eyes. The raw material is your optic nerve.

If you stare at a window or a rock for long enough you will see it is melting. Everything is moving. Everything is ghosted by afterimages of itself.

I love the Australian Aboriginal artist Yukultji Napangati. Napangati was part of the Pintupi Nine, a group of people who, to some white Western eyes, looked like they had walked out of the Paleolithic one day in the mid-1980s. Napangati paints the pathways of women foraging. Her work shimmers before your eyes like a forcefield or a heat haze. I cried when I first saw the painting called *Untitled* (2011). It was in the gallery of New South Wales in Sydney. I was with my friend Douglas Kahn, a sound scholar and sound artist and fan, like I am, of vibration.

Doug was crying too. That quality of forcefield, of things held in a soft shimmering tension, is the feel of electric peanuts.

Artists use materials. Painters use paint. But some painters like Napangati aren't just using paint. They're using you. I've also always loved the art of Bridget Riley. The moment at which I discovered electric peanuts was the moment I really started to look at her work in the Tate Gallery (now the Tate Britain). Bridget Riley's art materials are in fact your optic nerve. Those swirling lines in her paintings aren't exactly what you look at, they're not "objects" in that subject versus object sense. They're more like the words on this page or notes in a musical score. Your eye reads the score and the music is what happens in your optic nerve—a shimmering, cascading, oscillating movement.

Some of my friend Olafur Eliasson's work plays with afterimages. Recently he made tiny very bright fluorescent images of Earth. You stare at them and then you look away. Your eyes see the blue-green Earth we live on.

You can project the Earth, out of your own optic nerve.

It's empowering. It's why visualization is such a big deal if you learn to meditate. Instead of having images thrust upon you, you let them be evoked. The power of the "mind" (I dislike this word) to visualize is very precious indeed. In the end, it's what will help us imagine a future that is different from the godawful flames in which we now find ourselves.

Visualizing is a political act. When you're so beaten down that you can't even imagine a way out, you have lost the power to visualize, and the oppressor is winning. Electric peanuts don't look like much, they don't seem important at all. But perhaps their wispy flimsiness is another kind of power. Not the heavy Monty Python foot stamping on everything. A different sort of power, a spectral power. The power to open a gate to the future, to the possibility that things can be different.

The Marxist thinker Raymond Williams developed an intriguing idea called *structure of feeling*. It's related to this idea of shimmery power, or the power of shimmer. "Vague" and "cloudy" are exactly the progressive political qualities we find when we try to get a higher-resolution sense of structure of feeling. Structures of feeling are precisely vague and cloudy— they are like a chemical steam or liquid out of which precipitates crystals.

What are the crystals? They are *ideology*. What's that? Not just beliefs and attitudes but the whole way you live. And it contains cracks and contradictions, because the official labels in the record store of life that say things like *Ladies* or *Gentlemen* above doors were made in the past, and this isn't the past. There's always something else, shimmering.

Williams describes the structure of feeling of Welsh miners in the mid-nineteenth century. It's really a way of talking about their world. As I've argued in *Humankind*, "world" is never solid and smooth and perfectly bounded. Worlds are not like the smooth insides of coconuts. Worlds are more like string vests. Worlds are necessarily flimsy. That's how they can overlap, how we can share the world of a spider or another human being. Because of time, worlds can't be smooth and separate, one can't have a "full" world, and one can't have no world at all. There is always some kind of shimmer that we call time, so that when we try to point to "world" it disappears, like trying to catch water in our hands.

The structure of feeling isn't a thing you make up. You inhabit it. There are the mountains. There's the pit. This is how you do your job. Things are determined. You don't just make them up out of a void—the world is not completely constructed by a "subject." We are in a sense an "object" among others, but not in the way that you might hear that word. When you read the word *object*, you might think of objectification. But this kind of state depends upon a subject, a master. The subject versus object relation has always been about slavery.[1]

The first words out of my mouth as a baby were "pretty lights." Lights are things. Hallucinated lights are also things. Hallucinations are things. Ideas are things. Thoughts are things. We have this impression, this prejudice, that "thing" means "solid" or "lump" or "I can point to it" or "it's objective" or some mixture of these. We've been used so long to thinking, in white Western thought space, that there are "subjects" like us and then everything else is an "object." It's not hard to see, if you put it like that, how this actually implies that everything else is a slave.

The really nasty, oppressive thing about Aristotle's concept of a slave is that to be a slave is to be *organon empsychon*, a tool that just happens to have a soul. This is how some people still treat nonhuman beings such as "animals" (we need to abolish this word). *Don't mind that screaming sound they're making, it's just a mechanical noise.* A psychopath treats human beings like that. An "ecopath" treats the biosphere like that. Any subject-object dualism implies the ability to treat someone like that.

So if light can be an object, if a liquid can be an object, you might begin to see how objects aren't ready-made, pre-formatted lumps for your fingers to touch and your hands to hold and manipulate. Liquids slip out of your grasp. Light, you can't really touch it, not even if you're a subatomic particle. You can deflect it … but that's not the same thing. Thoughts—you can't point to where they are. If you point to your head you're just pointing at your head, they're not "in" there. Your brain is in there. And thoughts or ideas or hallucinations are things too. Alphonso Lingis calls a hallucination a *phantasm*.

Phenomenology doesn't mean what modern psychology says it means, namely "subjective experience." In that world, there's the actual process of brain firings happening. Then there's the phenomenology of it, which is fancy and technical for "how it feels, but that isn't really it." Edmund Husserl formalized phenomenology. His *Logical Investigations* are sort of like the relativity theory of philosophy, and Einstein and he are pretty much contemporaries. Husserl had an amazing idea. His idea was that logical propositions are independent of the minds that are having them. Logical propositions have to be, otherwise they couldn't be true. The way he proved it was very pleasant, I think. Imagine it's not true. Imagine you believe in a theory that logical propositions are actually symptoms of a healthy brain. You have a healthy brain, therefore you can think logically. This was a very popular idea in the nineteenth century, and it was called *psychologism*.

So then, what is a healthy brain? Well it's a thing you can observe using science. And what is science? Well, it's a way to make truths that can be proved logically. And what is logic? Well, it's a thing you can observe using a science. And what is science? Well, it's a way of coming up with truths that you can prove using logic. And what is logic. Why, it's a symptom of a healthy brain. And what is a healthy brain? Well, it's a thing that ...

See the problem? The argument is chasing itself around in a circle, not getting anywhere. So, Husserl reasoned, it can't be true! So logical propositions must be independent of the brains that are "having" them. You can say "If p and if p then q then q," or not say it, or never even have heard of it, and it's still true.

If your mind is an ocean, then logic is not the saltiness of the water. Logic is like a fish swimming about in that ocean.

And look at all the other fish! There's hoping, promising, loving, hating ... all the phenomena of one's mind. Tibetan Buddhism calls them *nangwa*. Very handily everything that isn't Buddha is *nangwa*. Toothbrushes, ideas about Buddha, the universe, this sentence—they're all *nangwa*. OOO calls them *objects*. That's it!

Me and my brothers and my six girl cousins, all of us staring at those electric peanuts. Maybe we all saw slightly different ones but none of them looked like whales or camels. They looked like peanuts. Or vajras. You see them with your eyes. I think we have the wrong idea about eyes. *Idea, eye* ... they're the same kind of word. An idea is an *eidos*, which is Greek for "a vision," something you can see. Something you can see because it's already there. This is basic Plato, folks. Talk about objectification. An idea is a thing that's already there before you see it. Then you say *I see*! You never say *I smell*! Or *I touch*! When you say *I hear*, it means you don't really believe whoever is speaking, or you understand them, but you're not buying into what they're saying. *I see* is king. With my mind's eye, I see something that's already there, clean, clear, sharply objectified in the bright light. What this isn't is a flickering pink phantasm in the darkness. What an *eidos* isn't is an electric peanut. Actually it's a paradox: whenever you try to visualize what it could be, that's not it. But real things you can see aren't like that. They're made of light, or clay, or feelings.

And they're not stable. They're fragile and evanescent. And that includes your eyes and the way you see things. Your eyes palpate things. That's because things are also palpating your eyes. That's one of my favorite things, an essay called "The Chiasm" by Maurice Merleau-Ponty. The chiasm means *chiasmus*, which means "cross." Only, if you see it from "above" it's an X where the two lines seem to touch in the middle. But if you look at it from the side you see that one line is below the other line, like two highways in Los Angeles. Intersecting, but not touching. The same, but different. It's really hard to imagine.

Patriarchy stole the eyes. We think the eyes are the same as what some people call "the gaze," which is how zombies look at you or how Cyclops the X-Man shoots a highly destructive beam from both eyes. This is about *alienated* eyes, eyes that have become abstract powers. I want to make up a new word: *eyelienation*.

Eyes are soft and wet and small. They have evolved about forty times over. They're a great example of how evolution doesn't have goals or end points—none at all, no matter where you look or at what scale you look. They're wet bags with light sensitive materials in them. Cells that respond to light must have existed before eyes. So, mysteriously, camouflage comes before vision! Hiding is why we can reveal. If not, everything would be visible and there would be no need to find anything out. Science would wither. Blindness is how we can see. We can see lamps because we can see electric peanuts. We can see because we can hallucinate.

2

Inner Bodyworker

My father died in 2020. My father was very strange. So strange, it's hard to describe. How violent he was, to himself and others. There are so many things to say about my father, and so many things I can't say. Not in public anyway. It would take too long and probably be too shocking. I have held this tension inside all my life.

Grief is the size of your life. It's the size of you. It's like having a huge, hard metal and stone sculpture inside, with all kinds of strange edges and shapes. I call mine *Barbara Hepworth*. It feels like a Barbara Hepworth sculpture inside me, a large, strange abstract shape with metal rods sticking out. Something that's as big as your life is impossible to see as a whole. You look around it ... the other side is so big that you lose sight of the side you started on. It's like trying to chase your tail. It's how you are, without "you." It's within you, without you.

The other huge grief I am feeling is about *geotrauma*. Geotrauma is now recognized as a psychological state that could benefit from psychotherapy. I spend my life talking in public and writing books and essays about ecology, and in particular the climate crisis facing the world. I write about terrible, scary things. And for the first time in my life, I really started to feel how terrible and scary these things are.

Emotions are like pieces of fruit in a bowl. The bowl is called grief. Grief is the biggest emotion. It contains all the others. It isn't necessarily sad, or even terrible. It has all these different colors and shades to it. Grief is bigger than all the other emotions. It can be very useful to stop violence, if you know that. Of course, if you don't, grief can be a huge cause of violence. But grief is bigger than fear. Fear is very short term, mostly. It's about what they call fight or flight. It has to do with hours, or days, or seconds. Grief has to do with years and decades. That's part of why it's bigger. Grief just has a bigger timescale. It's like grief is a piece of paper, and fear is a small stone. The piece of paper will always wrap around the stone.

Grief is like the afterimage of an emotion called panic. Panic comes from the Greek *pan*, meaning everything. Panic is the everything-emotion. Therefore it must contain joy, love, tenderness, along with terror and rage and fear. What a perfect duo for our times: panic, the feeling of 20/20 vision, 2020 was definitely like that. Grief, the lifescale aftermath of everything that has happened.

Panic is bigger than fear too. Fear is a way to tame panic. Fear puts up a wall and interrogates immigrants and tells you what is clean and what is dirty, what is natural and what is unnatural. Panic, it's the feel of dirty and clean, natural and unnatural, far and close, this year and the last ten thousand years, all colliding, all mashed together.

I'm the guitar. Grief is the guitarist, and the amp, and the pedals. Grief is the sound of the amp humming before grief slashes out a chord, and listens as the chord—whose name is panic—reverberates in the amp when she lifts her fingers off of me. Grief reverberates in the amp, dying to something a human ear can't hear.

Ideas come from feelings. Feelings are strange because they are not just symptoms of things that happened in the past. Feelings are from the future. Feelings are thoughts that you don't have words for, not yet. That's why you talk to a therapist or meditate or go for a walk . . . you want to know what this feeling is, what it is telling you. Ideas, on the other hand, are from the past. Ideas are feelings that you have figured out. Ideas are like receipts that come out of the cash register of the feeling process.

So the best way to do philosophy is to trust your feelings. Philosophy comes from your heart, not from your head. You don't want to shut the feeling down into a simple idea too fast. That would be like using a plastic fork and not a metal one. It's easy but it's not so great. So the best would be to let the feelings play out without quite knowing what they are.

This is not the same as saying we should abandon logic and reason. Far from it. We should be finding the logic in the feeling, the logical structure that it's made out of.

So the best would be to confront a feeling that is as big as possible. One that you can't get around, that you can't turn into a plastic fork. That would be like a nice long road with lots of lampposts on it—lots of ideas, a long journey. You have to keep going and not stare at the idea lampposts too carefully, or you could crash. Finally you are doing good philosophy that can help people and you aren't so arrogant about what you're thinking. You can't understand everything. You just can't. It's like being in love.

Grief would be the best emotion to work with as a philosopher, because you simply can't get to the end of it.

Grief is a bodyworker. Grief wants to give you a massage. Grief says, *Go on, just lie down, lie down in the fetal position and let me massage your abs. You will feel like you might throw up, then I will leave. And then I will come again. And again. And again. Drink water. We won't be stopping this now, not until you die. I'm here for you always.*

You live inside a whole series of ripples. Events are not dots on a line. Events are like ripples. They're in motion. Panic is the way all those ripples feel. Grief is the aftereffect. The afterimage. The electric peanut, if you like, of the brilliant flash we call panic.

I don't know how to solve this. I don't know if there is a way to solve this or if it's good to solve this. I think that it's very, very okay to be upset about what is happening. I think it's good for everyone to experience this, in the end. You realize that you are in your body, that there's no way to escape from that. There is no exit to the tunnel. It goes around in a circle, like how your body curls up in a ball on the bed and you cry. You can't get over grief. You let it get over you. You let it soften your ego.

Trinitite, it's a kind of crystal. A special grief crystal. I have a little piece of it on my shrine. I keep a lot of grief objects on my shrine. There's a thread from a car that my son Simon couldn't bear me to let go. There's a cup that my father gave me. There's a champagne glass from a relationship that didn't work out. Trinitite was formed in Trinity, New Mexico, when the first atom bomb exploded. Trinitite is evidence of a huge blast of panic.

My little piece of trinitite is glassy green on one side, roughened pink on the other. The rough side was facing away from the blast. The glassy side was facing towards the blast. There it is, that gigantic panic that caused Robert Oppenheimer to quote the Bhagavad Gita—"I am become death, destroyer of worlds." There it is, encoded into the obverse and reverse of a tiny sliver of green and terracotta.

Ecological awareness means making friends with the panic that comes from realizing we don't live on a thing that goes on and on and on forever and doesn't mind what we do to it, like the object of a sadistic fantasy. The "Fuck, I thought I was progressing, but really I was killing you, I feel the murder weapon warm in my hands, I thought it was a ploughshare, but it was always a sword."

But finitude is your friend, and grief is the feel of the handshake with that friend. OOO means that there is a beautiful finitude in reality. There is a gap in everything, even the universe. There's a crack in the universe, a very special crack because you can't point to it. It's ... I would say that it's "transcendental," but that might give you the wrong idea, that it's above or beyond or outside the physical universe. I would say that it's *subscendental*, which is my technical workaround for this problem—but then I'd have to explain it.[1]

There isn't a little dotted line on a thing and a scissors symbol saying *Cut Here*, to separate how a thing appears from what it actually is. Those two things are different, what a thing is and how it appears. Plato thought you could cut things to separate appearing from being. Racism thinks you can cut humans to separate real humans from subhumans. Patriarchy thinks you can cut gender to separate male from female. Nationalism, Nazism, incels . . . they're all about cutting the world into pieces.

You cannot cut grief into pieces.

3

Wimbledon Park Station

My clockwork alarm wakes me, 6am. That shrill, metallic drrrring. Very cold, my fingers malfunctioning, I get out of bed in my pajamas and kneel down before the gas fire. Each room has one. My mum can't afford central heating. Nor can she afford carpet. Most of the rooms have bare floorboards. I'm lucky, I have a thin light green carpet. I'm proud that it's a Wilton carpet. I have no idea what a Wilton carpet is. There's a hand-sized stain of Ribena, a blackcurrant juice squash drink, somewhere in the middle of the floor. It's 1979.

Click click click click BOOM. With a disconcerting flounce of flame, the gas fire ignites and its soft roar accompanies my getting dressed. My mum is still asleep. She's laid out my school clothes, folded, on my chair. I have a chair in front of a desk made out of a door. My grandfather tacked smooth thin board to it to make it a smooth surface, and solidly glued two huge cupboards on either size. It's colossal. I have a little train set, and a plant propagator, which in the end turns into an incubator for tadpoles and a home for stick insects. My tortoise, Merlin, has just died of cold—it was too cold in the house for him to hibernate alive.

I enter the dining room slash living room. There's a round table that my mum, Jasmine, inherited from her parents. It has a shiny, gaudy, somewhat wrinkled tablecloth from the 1970s—big flowers and bold colors. I enter the tiny kitchen and put the kettle on, put a teabag in a cup, and some bread in the toaster.

I'm ten years old and I'm getting ready to go to my new school. It's early and I'm scared and I'm utterly awake. It's 6:30am now. My mum enters, very tired, and kisses me good morning. Sparkler the ginger cat is asleep on a bean bag near the stairs to the back garden.

Buttered toast, tea. I brush my teeth in the little 1920s sink. Descend the staircase. Open the door to the lobby of our maisonette—there's a downstairs neighbor who shares this teeny lobby. I can't see the colors in the stained-glass window in the common front door. It's too dark. I exit. I pull the door and push it a little to make sure it's locked. I pat my left pocket—good, keys still in there. My keys are still in my left pocket as I type this. I pat my right pocket—good, there's my wallet and my season ticket for London Transport. I open the gate and turn right.

My wallet and keys have been in the same places since 1978.

I live right at the bottom of Arthur Road, right next to the railway lines. When I tell Californians where I grew up, I say that I grew up on the cover of Pink Floyd's *Animals*. Same railway lines, just a few miles south and west of Battersea Power Station.

Three blocks up the street is Wimbledon Park station. It's small and made of red bricks and it says *1889* on the front at the top. I'm alone, except for when I pass the Post Office. Outside is a red and white striped worker's shelter. I can smell the pleasant soft smell of molten tar. Someone in there is boiling some tea and reading the paper. The streetlights are still on. It's January. I'm about to get the tube to Hammersmith, a thirty-minute train ride. District Line from Wimbledon Park to Earl's Court, Piccadilly Line to Hammersmith, then you walk under the Tubeway to Lonsdale Road, then across Hammersmith Bridge. Finally the towpath, and the school.

I'm totally terrified. My mum doesn't have a car. I have to do this.

The ticket inspector asks me whether I've got a machine gun in my violin case. "Oh no. That's my sandwiches in there." He laughs. I don't know why. My mum told me to say it. I take it to be some kind of protective spell.

I'm too scared to take the bus. Bullies haunted the bus to my old school, Park House. The Tube feels safer—there's no people. But there are these sounds. These gigantic machines. These tunnels where the train often stops and waits. I'm usually alone in the second to the front carriage, for at least a few stops. I like very much being alone. Bad stuff might happen if I'm not alone. I sit in a very particular seat. Right hand side, facing forwards, on one of the sofa-like seats in the middle of the carriage, not the side-facing rows. If I don't get that seat, bad stuff will happen. I time my exit from the house so I can be sure to get a train with an empty carriage where I can secure that seat.

That train has nothing to do with me. I know that my obsessive compulsive behaviors are about the simple fact that the train carries on without me in mind, always. It's the stuff of life.

My grandfather's soul was on the seat, to my right, facing forwards, the middle of the old red 1979 District Line train to Upminster, the dusty smell of the carriage, the unfortunate smoky smell in the smoking carriage towards the back. The idea of Ken Livingstone, the very left-wing leader of what was then the Greater London Council—a couple of decades later he became Mayor of London. Margaret Thatcher abolished his position, and the entire GLC, because he was so left wing. Because, for example, he had decided that Tube fares should be flat and really cheap. I seem to remember that for one pound you could go anywhere at all on London Transport for a few months. It was absolutely amazing. It was a scheme called *Fare's Fair*. Brilliant. I've had season tickets and all sorts. The little ones and the larger ones that you fed into a machine.

I let the train take me into the underworld. For the first few stops, it's overground. Then it begins to travel through long dark tunnels. If it stops in the tunnel just before Earl's Court, my day will be destroyed.

Finally I get to Earl's Court. Now I'm down the escalator from the District Line, and I'm on the platform of the westbound Piccadilly Line. The look of an ad on that platform, for the film *Alien*. That egg, with a crooked glowing green-yellow smile at the bottom, and the caption: "In Space, No One Can Hear You Scream." It's a little piece of panic, pasted on the wall.

Stuck in a tunnel . . . T.S. Eliot has some lines about it in one of his *Four Quartets*. I read those on the Tube when I was about thirteen years old:

...when an underground train, in the tube, stops too long between stations

And the conversation rises and slowly fades into silence

And you see behind every face the mental emptiness deepen

Leaving only the growing terror of nothing to think about[.]

(East Coker, 3.18–21)

When a thing malfunctions you notice it. When it's functioning smoothly, it disappears. Even worse than my feelings in the tunnel before Earl's Court, if the Piccadilly Line from there to Hammersmith stopped in the tunnel as it was emerging towards a station called Baron's Court, I would lose my mind.

When life judders to a halt, you experience the basic anxiety called *alive*.

The tube train ascends from the underworld, near to Hammersmith Station. I walk down the underground tubeway as in Gary Numan's band, Tubeway Army. I still hear his "Cars" from this era, one of many earworms. Ironic really, because I didn't have cars. I had tubeways and the tube and bridges and the Thames.

An earworm is an electric peanut made of sound.

I'm returning from school at 4pm. I'm walking as fast as I can. I look really strange. The Thames looks scary. It's a while before the Thames Flood Barrier is erected and functioning. I'm crossing Hammersmith Bridge over water that still gives me nightmares, the river even wider than it is in real life, me about to fall in, half way across that bridge. It's ornate. I don't care. I'm marching at the double, cutting corners like a droid on a mission. That mission has nothing to do with looking like a cool or well-adjusted humanoid creature. Now I'm at the station, standing right at the back end of the platform, where I can get the same seat to Earl's Court, just two stops. The Piccadilly Line train glides to Baron's Court, then dives underground. I get out and go up the wooden escalator. It's often broken. The District Line waves melancholically and beautifully through a suburban world, leaves and bricks and bridges. Putney Bridge is scary. Parson's Green is sometimes flooded. It's below sea level by about three meters.

I return to Wimbledon Park station. It's all about afternoons now. There are flowers. I notice them. The same flowers were there earlier but it's a different time of day, a different set of emotions. I've made it home.

That was the pattern. The recipe. The algorithm. The past. It must've happened a good thousand or so times. I was an experimental plane pilot, training for spaceflight. The station said 1889 on the front. But really, it was a gate to the future. I still feel that way when I see train tracks. When I see a train coming around a leafy corner, like a machine emerging from a forest, those bright green and red lights like eyes. It's coming from the underworld. It's coming from the future. Wimbledon Park station was my NASA. I was training for flying to the USA. For life.

4

Oso

He's still here, on my bed, my teddy bear. My grandma gave me him on my first birthday. He was a lot bigger than me then. Now he fits snugly behind my shoulders or under my left arm while I'm sleeping. Yes. I sleep with my teddy.

He is called Oso because my grandma, whose name was Ruth, thought he was "Oh, so noble." But the way his name resembles the Spanish for *bear* strikes me more now that I live right next to Mexico. He has brilliantly orange eyes. I don't know what kinds of chemical were used in the late 1960s to make those eyes but you don't see eyes like that on a teddy any more. He used to have a red cardigan with his name emblazoned on it, in white. My grandma knitted it.

Oso used to be the ruler of a small tribe of soft toys. There was a koala. There was a green hippo. There was a black cat with brilliant green plastic eyes. There was a very eager looking creature of indistinct animal species, who is still with me. There was I think some kind of primate. There was a glove puppet Snoopy-like dog, called Sweep, based on a children's television show. I lost Sweep up the hill from my first house when I was about four and I was devastated. My mother went up the hill to look for him, in vain.

For quite a while I acted like I didn't need Oso. This was called my teens and my twenties. After about ten years of living in the USA, I realized I was wrong. I do feel a lot younger now or, as Bob Dylan puts it, "I was so much older then." There are so many messages about having to act like an adult. But, given how confused and violent so many of us are, what on earth is that as a model to live up or down to?

I get lonely and sad often, and it's nice to hold him in the night.

I like to understate. I have a strong desire to hold and be held . . . and Oso fits the bill very nicely. I look forward to it when I go to sleep.

Oso has sometimes been glimpsed hanging from a washing line in a garden. I was younger than ten, and my mum would point him out when I came downstairs, feeling sick. I must've thrown up all over him.

Soft toys, they used to call them. *Plushies*, it is now. The strange combination in that word of splashing and luxury seems wrong and indulgent. *Soft toy* is sterner by comparison, but at least it refers to the actual being in question. Plushy is an adjective to do with how they feel, like soft, but more so. That "y" at the end is a great example of a kind of mission creep that denies reality to the side of the entity itself . . . it strengthens the adjective *plush*—or rather it strengthens the adjectival quality, while weakening it in another way. Now it's *as if* they are plush. The "as if," fantasy quality is now to do with our human fingers. They're not even "toys"—just things that might, to our inevitably deluded senses, *feel* soft. Sometimes people say "stuffy" as in "stuffed animal." It's worse.

I don't like those words at all. Oso is not a plushy. Nor is he a stuffy. Oso is not reducible to his effects on me. Oso is a person in his own right. Oso is OOO.

And in a more trivial sense Oso simply isn't plush: he's firm and stout and has heavy, curly fur. He's not soft. He hasn't got much give. He doesn't *yield*. He's not an object in that master versus slave sense.

Hammer: it's a word that reduces a thing to its effects, a noun made out of a verb. Lots of words are like this. They are *metonymies*: nouns made out of things that the nouns do, or are made of, or look like. That's exactly part of why the n-word is intrinsically extremely violent. It reduces people to the way they appear to others. OOO is about resisting all that. It's about seeing how things are not just "for" us. They happen without us. Oso happens without me. That's why I love him.

Oso belongs to a family of things we call *inanimate objects*. That's a pejorative term in all kinds of ways. *Inanimate* is from Aristotle's division of things into animal, vegetable and mineral. According to Aristotle, animals are beings that move— they're "animated." Vegetables don't move, they just live. Minerals don't even live. In a way, for Aristotle, Oso is a kind of mineral.

Except we now know that plants do move. They just move differently than "animals." Actually we also know that things like crystals "move"—quantum theory tells us that everything is shimmering.

Oso now reminds me of my lizard Nicodemus. I can't speak about reptiles. I can't write about reptiles. I can't write about how wonderful they are. I can't describe what they do, because they confound language. I can't find a verb that is neither active nor passive. I can't find something in between doing and being. All I can do is use negative theology. *Apophasis*: the way of saying things by not saying them, un-saying ... non-saying. I'm not supposed to talk about lifeforms in this book. This book is supposed to be about "inanimate objects." But rules can be broken.

One reason for the rule is actually a feeling. It's a feeling of terrible grief. My lizard, a bearded dragon called Nicodemus, died in 2020. I tried to write about him, before and after his death. But I couldn't. He brought up so much sadness. So this is a book not-about Nicodemus. Which means that it is. Which means that I want to talk about him. This edge between book and non-book. This edge between alive and not alive.

I want to talk about lifeforms in this book that seems to be about "inanimate" things. I want to talk for a moment about lifeforms. I want to talk about beings who confound what we mean by "alive" and "animate." We think life is movement, and non-life is static. Reptiles are still. They aren't moving fast like a mammal. They aren't static like a pencil. They aren't moving in the way we like to think. Pencils and tulips aren't static in the way we like to think.

Nicodemus was so funny with my cat, Oliver. He could hypnotize Oliver by doing "nothing," just by looking like the rocks in his tank and standing still. Oliver would try to focus on him. Cats see in green and red quite a lot, and reptiles can take on the colors of the surfaces they exist on, like how artists can absorb things. So to Oliver, Nicodemus looked quite like a mottled reddish greenish rock. Oliver's eyes would cross as he tried to focus and he would go to sleep. Was this a "defense mechanism"? Biologists and nature show presenters like David Attenborough like to talk about how clever this is. Is it? It's not "stupid"—it's miraculous. But is it clever? We think stupid means *passive*, and we think clever means *active*. I can't speak about reptiles.

We have no way to describe what Nicodemus could do with Oliver. He was "doing" something amazing. He wasn't being "strong." But if I say "he was being weak" you will get the wrong idea and think I am scorning him. I can't praise him using patriarchal language.

It's like how hard it is to praise artists. They are doing something. Or are they? Nicodemus was like an artist in the way he blended with the rocks in his tank and hypnotized the viewer, Oliver, who looked at him the way I look at my beloved paintings of Bridget Riley and Yukultji Napangati.

Soft toys. Plushies. Children get to think of them as animate, as alive. The definition of adult is "someone who knows that's not true." My definition of that definition is, "someone who got wrapped around a lamppost and can't drive anymore, how sad." This idea that child means someone who's still allowed to talk to "inanimate objects" without being considered insane, it's everywhere. When something is everywhere, it means that thing is very old. Oxygen is everywhere. It comes from three and a half billion years ago.

I often tell my Ph.D. students that a dissertation is very much like a teddy bear. It's not something you buy in a shop, whether that shop be a medieval, capitalist or Soviet one. It's not a product, despite what neoliberal "professionalization" tells you. It's supposed to be well used and well loved, with stuffing coming out of its ears, covered in old vomit stains that have been partially cleaned off in the delicate cycle of a washing machine. I like to liberate my students from the idea that they have to act like they already have a job. This is very oppressive. It's getting worse. Nowadays they have to pretend as if they already have tenure— they've advanced far enough in their job to be making bigger and broader statements in shinier, and possibly higher-selling, products.

If we're going to go with the theory of J.W. Winnicott, someone like Oso is a "transitional object," something that gets you from early childhood to later childhood. I'm sure this isn't true of soft toys, and I'm sure it's not true of Ph.D. dissertations either. I think that in a way all objects are transitional, and not only for human beings. And that this doesn't mean that there's a progress from some kind of primitive A to a sophisticated B. What do I mean?

I learned a lot of these things from Oso.

Why should "progress" look rather brutal and serious, the basic model of a certain kind of patriarchal masculinity? Aliens are often depicted as closer to infants than we are, and there is some evolutionary truth in humans appearing more infantile than other primates. Perhaps the whole thing goes backwards. But I don't believe in unitary directions. True progress might look like regression. Lizards are in a sense failed tadpoles. Nietzsche wept when he saw a horse being beaten. It looked childish at the time. Nietzsche was right to weep. Now we would all weep.

The mysterious quality of a thing is the future. Oso is from the future. Oso exceeds me. He goes on without me. He sits on my bed when I'm not there.

5

Secret Door

There is a place called Cannizaro Park. It's next door to Wimbledon Common. It's strange. It's some kind of aristocrat's house from yesteryear. An out-of-date class mode. It has these huge ornamental gardens, somewhere between gardens and a park. There's a lake that looks like it belongs in India, it's hidden among trees, there are vines and gigantic leaves. I think of "Ride the snake / To the lake, the ancient lake," that line by Jim Morrison.

And further up there's a place where you go if you're having a picnic and you're in my family, and if I'm anywhere from five to fifteen years old. It's a place I walk to a lot on my own when I'm seventeen. There's a patch of grass there among the trees, and there's a big wall that surrounds the property. And in that wall there's a door. I was there a couple of years ago and I felt the same. *That's the door to another dimension.*

The park contains a lot of rhododendrons, a colonial favorite. They're also secret doors. Who knows where you could go if you entered one? I still feel this way. Trains do it to me, trains pulling out of stations and trains meandering down the tracks under the bridges near my childhood home, those sharp red and green lights in the twilight.

Behind the door? It's like a door on stage. There's no magical world behind it. There's a street behind it, with a pub. Down this street there is a place called Caesar's Well. It's in Wimbledon Common. It's quite hard to find. You walk past the ancient pub, The Fox and Grapes, past the golf course. It's just a hollow with some kind of grille. It's not really about Caesar, they just called it that for a couple of hundred years. It's from ancient Britain, and it might be a few thousand years old. It's some kind of portal. I'm sure of it.

The mystery that seems to lie behind the door actually floats *in front of the door*. It's in the feeling of "what is behind that door?" What is behind a door? The future. That's the real secret of a secret garden. It's not a past world. It's a world from the future. The Garden of Eden is just gaslighting. I learned all this from Cannizaro Park.

The mystery of the door includes the fact that we know there's nothing behind it. The door exists without us in mind.

There's a song by Laurie Anderson. It's called "Born, Never Asked." It has a wonderfully strange introduction, which sounds creepy:

It was a large room. Full of people. All kinds.
And they had all arrived at the same building
at more or less the same time.
And they were all free. And they were all

asking themselves the same question:

What is behind that curtain?[1]

Laurie has made a secret door out of a philosophical concept. This concept is the premise of a wonderful book about *distributive justice* by John Rawls. It's his image of "the veil of ignorance." You're given a choice of what world to live in, but you can't see that world yet, and you have no idea who you will be in that world. You are separated from the future by a veil of ignorance. Rawls argues that if you really don't know what will be behind the veil, it's very likely you will choose a world in which there is an equal distribution of wealth.

I love the phrase "that curtain." Suddenly it's there, this thing, you see it. It's creepy because it was already there, without our paying attention to it. It exists without us. It's "that curtain" that makes the song so powerful. You never hear of the curtain again. So it haunts everything.

African philosophy tells us that there are secret gates everywhere. Portals to hyperspace. They're everywhere, like right behind your sofa or inside your Christmas tree. I strongly approve of this idea. It's called Kalunga, a Kongo term for the gate between the worlds. It's amazing to me that the Kalunga looks like the inside of a spiral shell, that iridescent nacre . . . and that it's made of water. In other words, we've all seen it: it's the hyperspace tunnel in *Star Wars*. I love this idea that gates are everywhere. I want it to be true. I need it to be true.

My favorite work of art of the last ten years, by quite a long way, is a film by Khalil Joseph. It's for a tune called "Until the

Quiet Comes" by Flying Lotus.[2] The dance in this film is stunning: it's as if one of the characters is moving backwards, as if he is being filmed backwards ... but he isn't. He's moving forwards, but locking his body in such a way that it seems as if time has been reversed. What a utopian movement! Kalunga is a major character in this film. Joseph portrays it as aqua-colored water, looking spookily and disturbingly like the Atlantic into which so many African bodies were cast during the crossings of slave ships. This film shows you the power of imagery. There is no speech. It's just Flying Lotus's music. Despite the death in the film, a body rises from the dead, as if transported through the spirit world to our world via the gate, Kalunga.

The dancer climbs through the slightly opened window of a car, resting on its two left wheels, at an angle to the road. It's the angle of death, and the car is the chariot of death. For me it's the angle of death because of that skull in Holbein's painting, *The Ambassadors*, which I would adventure to find at the National Gallery in Trafalgar Square, every weekend of my teenage years.

I studied Hans Holbein's painting *The Ambassadors* for Art O Level in 1983. Holbein depicts two ambassadors surrounded by the trappings of wealth and power: a globe, a lute, some music, all kinds of opulence. But something is out of joint. There's a strange elongated shape rising at forty-five degrees from bottom right towards the center of the painting. When you look at it from the side, in a way that almost flattens the painting of the ambassadors and their possessions, you see that this weird cigar-shaped ghost is in fact a skull that has been stretched into a dimension that isn't in the picture plane at all. You have to ignore the normal rules of perspective, the stable "vanishing point" in front of which you need to stand so that the painting appears to be three-dimensional. When you see the skull for what it is, it's the ambassadors and all their worldly wealth and love and art that stretch and distort. In "Until the Quiet Comes," that car is the Holbein skull.

Holbein is making an amazing point about death: it's a whole other dimension, it's there but we don't see it, it bisects our world. Death is a secret door. The secret door in Cannizaro Park has haunted me, like a ghost, like an earworm, an electric peanut. A favorite 1970s children's TV program, *The Herbs*, was about a garden of talking plants, plants that had become lions (Parsley was his name) and dogs (Dill) and human beings (Constable Knapweed).[3] You reached this garden through a secret door. Then there were the Wombles from another TV show. The Wombles, large mousey beings who walk on two feet, made houses out of litter on Wimbledon Common, adjacent to Cannizaro Park. My dad played on Mike Batt's theme tune and (talking of nonhumans) he appeared as one of these Wombles on *Top of the Pops* when a spinoff song called "Remember You're a Womble" became a hit.[4] The door of their house was a dustbin (or trashcan) lid. A dustbin lid is a secret door, in the OOO sense. Because when you look at a dustbin lid, do you see a door? You'd have to remember you're a Womble to do that.

You'd have to remember that the world is not just a stage littered with your props for a play called *Human Beings Are the Only Reason Anything Exists and I'm Prepared to Burn Them to Cinders to Prove It*.

For Mike Batt's birthday party in 1976, my dad dressed as a punk and played in a string quartet in his garden. This was a time when punks were making skirts out of dustbin liners, so maybe remembering you're a Womble is not as hard as you might think.

I believe in them, these secret portals. I don't think my way of using or thinking about or accessing the world exhausts it. I think there are hidden corners, hiding in plain sight. The past and the future aren't totally distinct, they overlap. The future is right "here," just hidden. If you can just handle the thing you're facing right, if you know how to talk to it, maybe you will find it.

There are secret doors in your body, in your being. I study esoteric Buddhism, the kinds called Mahamudra ("the great symbol") and Dzogchen ("the great perfection"). The most secret door of all is your basic default being, right here, right now, hiding in plain sight. It's "self-secret," meaning that it's not exactly hiding, you can read all about it in your local bookstore or online, but ... there's a knack to opening it. Like jiggling a key in a lock just right. But you can do it. You can jiggle that key—the instructions for jiggling are called *upadesha* in Sanskrit, which mean, "secret (there's that word again) aural instructions." It's like finding a secret door on the side of your neck that you never knew was there. If you open it, this amazing thing happens. You discover your Buddha nature. Then you have to keep on and on discovering it for the rest of your life. That's the tricky part.

Buddhism and OOO are quite, quite compatible. In a way, meditation is letting your "mind" just be, namely, just to be mysteriously and effortlessly itself. It is acknowledging the basic "withdrawn" aspect of the mind, by which is meant its secret, mysterious, unspeakable quality. Mysterious comes from the Greek *muein*, which means "to close the lips," in other words, *mmmm*. Like I said a while back, I don't like that word, *mind*. So much Buddhist literature in translation contains the word. It automatically makes white Western people snap into a default Cartesianism: mind versus body. And this is absolutely not the flavor of the original. It would be better, I think, to say *soul* as I've been saying it here. What does your soul "look like"? It's a tune by DJ Shadow: "What Does Your Soul Look Like?"[5] It's like that Zen koan, "What was your face before you were born?" Hint: the question is the answer.

I think the world would be in better shape if we humans could let things be secret like that door in Cannizaro Park. Not hidden away, guiltily concealed, not lies or terrible truths. Just ... you know, you're walking down the street with your Person, and you give each other that look, and it doesn't matter that no one else can see, and it doesn't matter that you can't wrap your head around it.

I think poems are like that, and novels and plays and paintings and ... I think they have secret doors. My basic tactic for reading is, locate the door to utopia. Make it wider so that everyone can see it. Fly through it with as many people as you can muster. I recently set this exercise as the last piece of work for a class I was teaching at Rice University on propaganda. Some students smiled.

This secret door thing. It might just be a strong case of trying to see the good in everything, which isn't as great as finding the secret door. But sometimes this door is very different from the rest of the art. The artist may not have put it in there on purpose. It might totally disrupt the rest of the art. That's okay. That's great, in fact.

The door in Cannizaro Park opens onto a street with a wall in it. But don't let that fool you. It is a portal.

6

CPAP

I'm awake, and I'm panicking. I can't breathe. More than that: I'm having asthma. More than that—fuck, am I choking on acid reflux? Yes I am. There's a strange sound, it sounds like a goat shouting. It's me breathing—breathing out, but finding it impossible to breathe in. I think I might die. What can I do . . . let's try to get my inhaler. Where is it . . . wait . . . I can't move. I've woken up smack in the middle of REM sleep and I have sleep paralysis.

I'm crawling towards the bathroom. There's a chair on which I know my trousers are lying. My inhaler is in there. I must've made it, and used the inhaler, because I'm writing this now.

It's shocking and horrible. But the dream I was having just before it, or was it a dream . . . I see the tunnel, and the light at the end of it. I see my Buddhist meditation teacher. We are in a huge hotel ballroom. He points upwards and says, "Everyone look up at the chandelier. . ." It's a huge, gaudy, glittering chandelier. It is emitting a strange swishing sound, the tinkling of the glass mixed with something else, but what? The sound gets louder and louder and as I look at it, I start to be sucked upwards into it. The sound increases to a kind of ripping like paper or fire or tearing metal. Then I find myself in a velvet darkness, very relieved and very excited . . . this is going to be meditating with my teacher for the rest of time! There are several people here . . . I can't see their faces, maybe they don't have them. We are all wearing cowls like the Sith in *Star Wars*. That's when I wake up, doing a Jimi Hendrix, choking on acid reflux.

I have had a few of these "near death experiences." Aficionados call them NDEs. I think I've had about fifty. I don't know what they are or why they happen, but I know that they're always the same. There's the giant, glittering, roaring mandala, the chandelier in that one dream, a kind of chrysanthemum of light, "the light at the end of the tunnel." There's the being sucked through it into a totally different reality. There are these other people on the other side. Terence McKenna calls them "elves." My mind interprets them as humans, and as meditators, maybe because it's just reaching for stuff it already knows. Maybe they're not really human.

Maybe it's not a dream.

To try to understand what was happening, I read a book about the chemical called DMT.[1] DMT is the most powerful psychedelic substance on the planet, and it's everywhere—it's in the grass outside the window here . . . it's in your brain. Everyone who tries DMT via smoking or injection seems to have the exact same experience, the one we summarily call "the light at the end of the tunnel." The book was arguing, what if that was what happened when you're dying? What if your brain dumps a lot of its DMT as you start to die, for some reason? Could it be a door or Kalunga between this world and another one? I've had a few psychedelic experiences, with and without drugs, but this was very powerful, it involved almost actually dying, and it was produced seemingly by my own body. Without me. Within me, but without "me."

There must be something in my brain that's obsessed with my throat closing, like how your fingers can get obsessed with rolling paper into little balls. Or pretending to. "Pill-rolling" I think they call it, in psychology. Part of me must get some pleasure from the way the skin in my throat can be compressed to touch itself. Who cares if Tim Morton dies . . . certainly not my brain.

So I got a CPAP. I was about forty years old. It's a machine that makes you breathe right. It forces air into your nose. It sounds invasive, but it feels blissful. After years of waking up choking and nearly dying, I'm happy that oxygen exists.

My CPAP looks like a large white lozenge, with a big button, just one, at the top. It turns the thing on and off. When it's on, it just pumps the air in the room into my lungs at a rate of eight cubic centimeters per second. That's like a medium-sized flow of water from a tap in your kitchen sink: about as thick as the barrel of a felt tip pen. That sounds scary, like I said, but trust me, it's an immense relief. The CPAP looks so simple but it's filled with sensors that detect when my breathing stops or becomes erratic, then it forces more air into my lungs. It contains a chip that the sleep study center at my health care place can analyze. It keeps a record of how long I sleep and what kinds of breathing I am doing.

When I first started to use it, I felt like a cork bobbing up and down on a gigantic ocean of oxygen. I felt so terrible before I got the machine. I felt like there was something very wrong with me. I felt abject. Now I'm glad I identify as disabled—I have sleep apnea and I have major depression. If it weren't for the prosthetic devices of pills and CPAPs, I'd be dead by now. I remember the person who fitted it, it was somewhere in Sacramento, California, and she said, "Even now as you sit and test the machine, you will feel relief." It was a kind of incantation. Her tone was so meaningful and soft and firm. She was right.

It's weird that a machine cares more about my breathing than I do. That it continues my life, without me.

I use my CPAP every night. I have to or I would wake up choking to death. It's a little bit sad not to have those NDE dreams anymore. But honestly, oxygen is great if you're not an anaerobic bacterium. The initial rush of air into my lungs is so soothing. The machine looks like a brick of white plastic. But it's covered in sensors that monitor your breathing and all kinds of things. It sends the information to the doctor. It tells you how much you slept the previous night and whether you had any instances of stopping breathing.

The CPAP made my career take off. I could think and write and speak and not collapse in the middle of the day after drinking six very strong cups of coffee, finding it impossible to be on time or go to sleep. The machine also made me realize that I have a disability, and this encouraged me to think about how every eye is an artificial eye, every leg is a crutch or a prosthetic leg. I'm very grateful to my CPAP.

The default art is dance. And the default of dance is called "alive." And the default of "alive" is being asleep. And the default of being asleep is the REM state where your body is in total paralysis and your brain is rippling with the things we call dreams, and your heart and lungs and all those squishy things are going squish, squish, squish. The stillness inside the stillness inside the stillness. Still doesn't mean static. It changes our idea of what moving is, that word does, if you think about it. Still, thrill. Still can mean "carrying on" as well as "not moving" ... there's the clue. Still is to stasis as quiet is to silence.

I think that's a precious state. I think that Black Lives Matter is talking about just this state of "alive." Black Lives Matter, it's a sentence from the future. Wouldn't it be great if they did? Wouldn't it be great for a Black person to walk down a street not afraid of violence and murder? Just alive, just being alive, breathing. Your heart pumping.

The Greeks used to call this kind of "life" *thumos*. It's not life as in "what's different about a plant compared with a pencil?" It's not life as in some legal definition of what you can do to a lifeform (the idea of "bare life"). It's not *bios* (the biological concept) and it's not *zoe* (the juridical one). The Greeks had other words for those kinds of life. *Thumos*, it's where the second syllable of *rhythm* comes from. When you say "thumos," you point to your chest. I just saw my daughter's heart, pulsing on the screen of an echocardiogram. The room was dark. I was crying. It was even more amazing than seeing her in her mother's uterus. It was a pulsing, trembling opal, filled with holes. The technician was adding color so that he could see it better. Thirty-three little movies of my daughter's heart ended up on that technician's screen. As it swiveled and vibrated, the heart flashed with color. I thought of some lines of Coleridge:

Blue, glossy green and velvet black
They coiled and swam, and every track
Was a flash of golden fire.

(*The Rime of the Ancient Mariner*, 279–281)[2]

The Ancient Mariner is admiring the water snakes. The snakes are somewhere between disgusting and beautiful, somewhere called alive. Writhing and curling in the water, they cause the Mariner to exclaim "Oh happy living things!" (282). I think you must feel that if you're a biologist. It must be what gets you out of bed and back to the lab.

I'm glad it's what I write about, *thumos*. I'm glad it's where I've landed. *Thumos*, the trembling of the body without any deliberation or intent. It's also a feeling of wonderment or strangeness or expectation. You can feel it when you meditate. You can also feel it when you're studying what they call "theory." It's that feeling of electrical uncertainty. I'm sure that "alive" is actually the feel of theory class, when you really think about "life." They used to say literature was all about it. Then theory class dismissed that, very brilliantly and for me effectively, and with good reasons. But really, they go together, as I'm starting to find. This open-ended "What if?" quality is very precious. What if I was wrong? What if we didn't have to live like this?

The *rhy–* part of *rhythm* means body fluids, as in the word *diarrhea*. The *–thm* part comes from the Greek *thumos*, which means core, heart, pulsation. We too often confuse rhythm with the *measurement* of rhythm, in a weird infinite regress. No one ever stops to wonder what the word actually means. I'm glad my CPAP has kept me breathing long enough for me to realize.

Aldous Huxley coined a word for substances such as psilocybin and LSD and DMT, a word far better than *psychedelic*. Psychedelic was coined because some alcoholics were scared straight by LSD, in what they assumed was an encounter with God. Psychedelic means "revealing the soul," as if the appearances of this world were a mere veil that must be burned off. Think of the violence this idea has caused, the nihilism, the fatalism. The appearances of this world are not simply a veil. It's much more mysterious than that. The appearances of this world, the data of the world, are just exactly how real things appear. The phenomena we call reality are not secret doors to something more real. Remember? The mystery is on *this* side of the door. We can't get at the things in themselves, we can only get at the data. Which means that we are stuck with the possibility that the data might be false, might be an illusion. This feeling of irresolvable uncertainty is the true feeling of being a scientist.

Aldous Huxley decided that substances such as mescalin were to be called *phanerothyme*. *Phanerothyme* comes from the Greek word *phainesthai*, to appear, and *thumos*, life. Phanerothyme means "life-display," the appearing of life as such. Pulsation made manifest. A CPAP for the soul.

7

Antidepressants

I can't move ... I can't move without another avalanche happening. An avalanche of sensations, thoughts, emotions, memories. All of them so vivid, all so poignant, so sharp—poignant, pricking you like the point of a knife.

I'm bending down, I'm crouching near the chest of drawers, I'm trying to remember why I'm here ... I'm trying to find a pair of socks, that must be it. The avalanche is getting in the way of remembering. Everything else is happening. And I can't think straight—I'm really angry with myself, distressed and angry, that I can't think straight. And I can't remember very well, in fact I suddenly realize that I can only remember about five minutes into the past. And I can only project about five minutes into the future. Finding these socks is turning into a major Arctic expedition.

I think I might be more scared than Whiskers the cat. I know I'm more scared than Whiskers the cat. I'm more scared than Whiskers the cat. Oh God ... I picture Whiskers coming up and pressing his head against my leg out of empathy.

It's December 2013, I am having suicidal thoughts every five minutes. There's that five-minute metric again. It might've been more like one or two minutes for memory, anticipation, and suicide. I'm saying "five" because it sounds like a small enough molecule of time. Suicidal thoughts are funny. They just pop in your head, like logical propositions or electric peanuts, even if you think you're the sort of person who would never do that. The magic words to say to the doctor if you're reading this and you think you might need the pills are "suicidal ideation." Just popping in your head—that's what "ideation" means.

One week later, I swallow my first Bupropion pill, and all that started to shift. Bupropion boosts your dopamine. I don't really know what that means. I think that dopamine is the neurotransmitter that says "Well done!" when you eat some butter. Cholesterol, a mental health chemical. I remember almost eliminating cholesterol because I had a medical issue, in about 2010. I remember feeling really sick after a few months and then deciding to eat some. So I ordered some fish soup at a restaurant in Bodega Bay, where Hitchcock set *The Birds*. One spoonful later I was in a state of hyperbliss. I realized what Siddhartha might have felt when, after months of self-flagellation and setting himself on fire, he deigned to have a spoonful of the rice pudding that an elderly lady had kindly given him. *Pleasure is the pathway*, he realized, quickly abandoning Hindu asceticism.

Those little Bupropion pills are like the old saccharin tablets, or cake decorations made of smooth opaque white stuff. They're coated with something that makes the chemical release quite slowly into your bloodstream. The first few weeks I was taking it, it wasn't in that form. They were little green lozenges. The depression would snaffle them right up and I would be back to square one within a few hours. First my psychiatrist tried increasing the dose of the regular pills. That still didn't work. Finally she put me on the little white slow-release ones, and the maximum dose of Bupropion that you can take—yeah, I have severe depression. It worked. It worked without me.

But even those weaker pills worked a little, those first few days. It was a vivid contrast. I was walking out of a hardware store with my kids. I felt a little tiny bit carefree. I hadn't felt that for months. Half a year, really. In bed later that night, I could close my eyes and rest. I had been jumping out of my skin at the slightest sound.

I had stopped taking Lexapro in 2012; in the UK it's called Cipralex. Lexapro is an SSRI, a selective serotonin uptake inhibitor. It tells your brain not to snaffle up all that serotonin. I had just arrived in Houston, and I had a new doctor—I was about twice his age. He was so brusque and uncaring—basically he had just gotten out of medical school. He had told me that a certain migraine pill I use (which is also an SSRI) interacted badly with Lexapro, increasing the risk of seizure. I questioned him. My previous doctor had never given me that impression: he was new, she was experienced. Unthinkingly, he needed to be right and without even talking or looking at me he printed out a form that corroborated this and handed it to me. A year later, I was going along with him. Maybe stopping Lexapro would help me lose weight.

But I didn't want to see a psychiatrist. That would be to admit that I really did have a problem. Maybe that previous doctor wasn't right—she was after all my GP, not a psychiatrist.

A year later, when the psychiatrist found out about what had happened, she was pretty shocked.

When you stop taking an antidepressant you have to "taper" the dose, decreasing it gradually so your body gets used to it slowly. But it's not pleasant however you do it. For the first few months of 2013 I had felt little clicks and pops in my head. They're part of "pruning"—your brain is literally eliminating various connections, and you can feel it. It's quite unnerving. You're teaching, and at the same time your brain is clicking. You're teaching, and you're starting to feel a bit anxious. But you can handle yourself. You're a meditator. You're a survivor. Come on, you've been in psychoanalysis for sixteen years! You know the difference between your mind and your brain! What could go wrong?

Everything could go wrong. No, you don't know the difference between your mind and your brain. As you get more and more depressed—2013 was one long, huge, intense depressive episode (that's the technical term, "major depressive episode" in fact)—you just believe what's in your head. Your brain starts to rewire. It confirms the loops then loops some more. What I'm saying is, one thing at least, if you feel even ten percent of what I was feeling by half way through 2013, please, please, *please* take antidepressants. Please.

When you first take it, Bupropion makes you feel like you inhabit your body. You feel comfortable in your body. In a state of depression, you just can't get comfy at all. Everything has sharp edges. But it's not as if the Bupropion is numbing you out. It's hard to describe if you haven't tried it. I've been taking three

150mg tablets of the stuff each day since 2013: like I said, the maximum dose. That's almost ten years. My psychiatrist tells me, I mustn't stop taking it now. I've had too many depressive episodes for that to be safe.

Bupropion cares about my brain by flooding it with neurotransmitters, the same way the CPAP cares about my brain, by flooding it with oxygen. My mind doesn't seem to care much for my brain. I am now on the side of my brain, the object-quality of my mind, the actual thing from which my mind arises.

Several of you are now going to stop reading this because you think I'm crazy. Thanks for continuing if you're continuing—you might be continuing *because* you think I'm crazy, but that's just fine. I am crazy, crazy in terms of a Western medicine diagnosis, even: I have major depression with anxiety. In fact I am a textbook case. I got A+ on the depression test, and A on the anxiety one. The psychiatrist I started to see in January 2014 had never seen a depression score that high.

I still don't think depression is a "thing," though. Depression is a list of symptoms. So is schizophrenia, which my brother Steve has. The pills they give you for depression work on the symptoms, not the cause. In a way, depression is a mode your being can be in. Western medicine used to believe in subtle fluids and modes: they called them the *humors*. There were four of them: blood, phlegm, black bile and yellow bile. Melancholy (depression) was the mode of black bile. Couldn't agree more. For a start, it's definitely not just thoughts. Sorry, cognitive behavioral therapy, but you're never going to convince me that emotions are just distorted thoughts. CBT was perfected in ex-gay therapy. (I note

with some grim humor that CBT also refers to the BDSM
practice of causing pain to the male genitals.)

Depression seems to be about the intellect. There's a difference
between intellect and intelligence. The "-ence" part of intelligence
is the tail that wags the dog. The suffix means roughly that
intelligence is a feeling. Wisdom is a feeling. It's definitely not a set
of ideas. I will keep on insisting that wisdom is a feeling. People
do get that wrong about "philosophy," don't they? It's two
emotions, people! It's love and wisdom. Loving wisdom. An
emotion about an emotion. Intelligence doesn't mean you have a
high IQ. Intelligence means you can make a joke or get a joke or
have an idea—or whatever you want to call that, they're exactly
the same thing as far as I'm concerned. Making jokes and having
ideas versus crying with despair and feeling suicidal. There's a big
difference between intelligence and intellect.

Intelligence is like clothes: why you wear them, how you wear
them, buying them, making them, showing off your style with them.
Intellect is like folding the laundry. You don't buy clothes just to fold
them and put them in a chest of drawers. If laundry folding was in
charge of buying clothes, you'd be naked. It would be more efficient
that way. If intellect was in charge of intelligence, killing yourself
would be the ultimate logical conclusion of any thought process. It's
more efficient that way. Just read a bunch of philosophy: *Why should
I not kill myself?* is right up there in the popular philosophy questions
Top Ten. In a way, if philosophy really is about emotion and
intelligence, a whole lot of it is devoted to talking you down.

Like I've said before, logic is like folding the laundry. You
don't like how you fold the laundry or where you put it? You're

welcome to invent another way and use a different kind of storage. You don't like what vanilla patriarchal logic, with its Law of Noncontradiction, does to you and the world? You're totally welcome to invent another one. That law, by the way, has never been proved, just like it's never been proved that you need to roll your socks together into those balls. Probably for the same reason (can I put the "weeping with laughter" emoji in this book?). It's just something that some people like, and some people insist that you do. For me at any rate, *contradictory* can be a serious symptom of *true*.

But you don't wear clothes in order to fold laundry, and you don't like philosophy just to wield your logical weapons. And you don't get to believe your intellect. That would be like believing that the guy who rolls their socks into balls must be right. Or in fact better than you. Depression is, I think, an allergic reaction of your intellect to its host being: yourself, or better, your soul. Intellect is always looking for anomalies. Very often these anomalies, given a bit of violence, can harden into the binaries and non-contradictory "truths" that we know and love. But it doesn't have to go that far to hurt. That's because the host of the intellect, you, is one huge anomaly.

You're an evolution product that arose from random mutation, so you're covered in bits that don't make much sense. Ears don't make sense compared with iPhone microphones. If evolution was about making sense, a few billion years of it would definitely have given us little tiny dots for ears. And you're a life product that arose from years and years of highly contingent stuff happening. Contingency has the same sort of meaning as "randomness." I think we should ban the word "deserve." I don't deserve to be mildly successful. It just happened. It could easily have been someone else. It was "random." If you believe you deserve the good stuff, then you also deserve the bad stuff. Think about the extreme version, where it's your fault that you were born poor, like in the Indian caste system.

And even more deeply, you're an ontological product from a principle that you don't coincide with how you appear. Talk about anomalies. Even an iPhone that just made it out of the factory is that kind of anomaly. I've been talking in this book about how this anomaly is the difference between your *self* and your *soul*. The soul is the whole of you, that you can never totally see.

The intellect thinks it can see everything, and it doesn't know when to stop. That means that it may never stop in some people. And just as an allergic reaction can end in a fatal anaphylactic shock if it's really extreme, depression can end in suicide. If you have extreme depression you need extreme intelligence in that moment not to do it. It's totally logical. It would end all the pain, even (you reason) for those around you, to whom you have (you reason) become or always were insufferable.

It's like tragedy versus comedy. Tragedy is just a small twisted region of comedy space that thinks it's everything. If you watch one person going through the motions like the Catholic priest in the Mass (so you don't have to—tragedy is somewhat automated this way), trying to escape the web of fate only to find that this makes the web even tighter, it's called *Oedipus Tyrannus*. But when you see eight people doing that, it's called *Curb Your*

Enthusiasm. And you're not rubbernecking them like they're special and different. You are somehow involved, much more directly. Comedy doesn't mean the opposite of painful or sad things. Comedy is more like a spacious meadow that can contain all those emotions, like a nice habitat for them, where the emotions don't eat one another. In a tragedy "fear and pity" (or whatever) eat everything else. Tragedy is the intellect thinking it's the main character and getting away with it. Comedy is where that might happen a bit, but in the end, the laundry folder realizes they're just there to fold the laundry, and there's more to life. I say to my intellect that I know it could break out in extreme violence at any moment—this seems to be how to keep myself safe. To realize that at any moment, I could weaponize the way I'm thinking. Anything can be weaponized, you know. I've seen Jason Bourne in the movies, using a biro as a knife.[1] It's safe to know that.

A few days after starting on the antidepressants I had a dream. I met my depression, personified as a version of myself. This version was the kind of self my intellect could live with. No matter whether the intellect could really get along with this guy, this guy was definitely better than me. My depression self was slightly taller than me, slightly smarter, slightly wittier, slightly more handsome, with slightly darker hair. Why couldn't I be more like that? (The main reason is, I'm not that. That fact could be fatal. Read on.)

My depression self was sitting next to me at a banquet. We were having a banquet at a long table near a canal in Venice. Outside . . . the night air, the sound of water slapping the gondolas gently. There were eight or so others, chatting and passing the wine. What happened was this: this cooler version of me would talk with me, then the dream would reset, mutating over and over until I woke up. In version one of the dream, the depression version was telling me that he loved everything I wrote, that I was amazing. Then the dream reset. In version two, "I really, really like this thing that you wrote on page x of your book y." Version three: "You're so wonderful. But I do have a question about this one thing you say on this page of that book." Version four: "I don't really agree with what you say on this page, although I think the whole thing is great—there are one or two flaws." Version five: "I'm afraid I have a serious disagreement with some of your ideas. A lot of what you do is pretty good, but . . . ." Version nine: "It's not just the dreadful mistakes you've made in your work. You yourself are a dreadful mistake. You should kill yourself. You should jump into the canal and drown, right now, in front of everyone here. You're a total disgrace who should never have existed."

Very, very luckily (thanks intelligence) this was when I started to become aware that I was dreaming, like that moment in *Alice in Wonderland* when Alice realizes that the people torturing her at this show trial are "nothing but a pack of cards."[2] Or like the "recognition scene," but comedy style. I think everything Aristotle said about tragedy he also said, or you could say, about comedy. There is comic hamartia (comic flaws), comic hubris or acting out, comic catharsis—laughter, and those moments of tearful release. And there is comic anagnorisis or recognition. My favorite is the end of Shakespeare's *Comedy of Errors*. The acting out gets so intense that real physical violence, possibly murder, is on the cards. Then suddenly the play wipes it all, with five minutes that always make me cry: "Oh my god, I'm your wife ... oh my god, I'm your son ... oh my god, I'm your brother ..."

The comedy of errors. What a beautiful title. Errors, like making mistakes. Errors, like wandering and contingency. How realizing that making errors isn't the end of the world—it might be the beginning of the world, and it might be impossible not to make mistakes. You might be a mistake, and that might be the best thing about you. To act is to err. This is built into OOO. Since acting is a way of appearing, and appearances never coincide with things in themselves, then every action is a failure, a pratfall, a misdirection or sleight of hand.

Birth is a rare form of abortion. No, it really is. The embryo is trying to suck the life out of the mother's body. The mother's body is quite rightly trying to eject the foreign object. Only the placenta mediates the standoff, and that's only because it's a product of a retrovirus called ERV-3 that lives in your DNA if you're a mammal. The smooth coat of the placenta is like nothing more than the smooth protein coat of a virus. The smoothness stops pathogens but it also stops white blood cells and it stops the embryo from literally sucking everything.[3] Symbiosis includes this kind of uneasy standoff. Things need to be uneasy to be safe. Safety is a rare form of uneasiness.

Or you could build a totally solid wall and interrogate everyone who comes in and deport most of them to a dangerous country.

I love those moments of recognition in comedy. Recognition of what? That you're a frail failure called a lifeform. *Oh my goodness, you're my dad* means, *I was born*. Talking of feelings, it's called "emptiness" in Buddhism and emptiness is most definitely not a concept. It's definitely a feeling, that feeling of "aha!" or "ahhh"—realization and relief. The Sanskrit "seed syllable" for emptiness is AH. Go figure.

I realized it was a dream, while I was starting to speak to this depression self: "I'm really sorry [wow, classic depression mind, apologizing even there, in that moment], but I can't. I don't want to. I've got kids. And I want to live."

It wasn't until I woke up, covered in sweat with goosebumps of horror all over my body, that I realized I had just met my depression self. And told him to fuck off. Bupropion supports my brain. I certainly don't often seem to care about my brain. But if my brain collapsed, I would collapse. My brain is "me" without my idea of "me." These days, I am a big fan of my brain.

8

Concealer

"You're standing wrong."

He was quietly rasping it right into my left ear. I was standing, right or wrong, on an Underground station platform. It was 2002.

I'm holding my concealer stick. It's the size of a nice fat felt tip pen, and it's made by Kat von D, and has gothic lettering. The top pulls off with a satisfying suck. There's a little wand attached to it that you pull out. It's coated with concealer.

You put your sunscreen and tinted moisturizer on. Then you smear on some mattifying cream. It covers the shiny parts of your face, making it all smooth and sheer. Then with a brush you coat your face with foundation powder. Not too much. You want to let your face shine out. Then out comes the concealer stick, and you dab it on.

My concealer is a pale creamy color. You dab the dots of concealer with a wedge of silicone, a "beauty blender," and suddenly your face begins to look . . . like what? There is a feeling of power. A feeling of "together." A feeling of I could now take on the world.

It's when the concealer goes on that I start to feel "normal." I start to smile. To feel good about myself. This little stick of concealer is very benevolent. The idea that your un-made-up face is the real you is overrated. The Greek for *face* is also the Greek for *mask*. Same in Latin. That's because we always only ever see facial data. We never see actual faces in themselves. So why not play with your appearance? Why does there have to be this patriarchal concept that there is a genuine, totally transparent being under there, a being often called Man?

OOO holds that there are no transparent anythings. Everything is hiding behind its own version of concealer stick, and concealer is always tinted. Concealer is bringing out something within me. Or is it revealing something without me? I love the ambiguity.

You're standing wrong. It was his proximity that disturbed me more than what he said. Recently I've figured out why. I wasn't standing in open hostility to English mores. For example, I wasn't standing "wide," the thing people call the "power stance." I wasn't standing like a cowboy in a frozen swagger. In fact that was part of the trouble. I wasn't standing wide enough, because *wide* means *male*.

I was standing feminine.

I'm the kind of girl who phones his mum every day,
But I don't fancy boys.

I made up that poem in 2020. That year was when I found out, thanks to a very kind helpful person, that I am non-binary.

I knew I was immediately. I had dreams about it. I cried about it. I was amazed about it. I couldn't stop thinking about it. I bought clothes about it. And makeup. And so this chapter is about a stick of concealer, in particular a quite goth concealer by Kat von D, if you must know. I'm pretty pale.

I didn't even like the term before I realized that if the shoe fits . . . I was suspicious of the whole thing, but for no good reason at all. We are told online and by looking at Pride flags that gender is a spectrum. It implies there's a smooth continuum. But maybe there isn't. I don't know. Who am I to say? Especially now that I have this feeling. Feelings as I keep saying are from the future. You don't know what they're telling you yet. That's what's so amazing about them. I would rather stick with this feeling, and the label "non-binary," than try to figure it all out, right now, thanks very much.

I'm non-binary. You would've thought such things are obvious, but at least to me they weren't until 2020. It is really quite peculiar that a disruptive virus that forced humans to have a global perspective occurred in a year whose number is associated with perfect eyesight . . . Maybe also because I'm intellectual and because I'm a survivor I can hold on to ideas for grim death long past their use-by date. That's the past casting its long shadow over today. I don't like it. I want to live now.

I'm a feminist, I know that much. Always have been—I learned a lot from my mum and my eldest cousin, Lexi.

"You're standing wrong." I was waiting for the Victoria Line, it's one of my favorites. I've loved the Underground since I was little, like I say. I was at the end of the platform, listening to the roar of the trains in the tunnels. *You're standing wrong.*

Is it that obvious? I thought. Meaning: *Am I so American now that I'm standing with some kind of wide swagger?* Am I standing too American? Have I, in the words of *Happy Days*, jumped the shark and actually started becoming assimilated into the US of A's collective of loud-mouthed, explicit rudeness? At the time I wanted desperately to return to the UK, and this comment made me feel that finally I didn't' belong, like it or not, America was in the very way I stood, and an officious Brit (as I had started to call them to my American friends) was correcting my manners in public. It seemed plausible.

Then, more recently . . . Wait a second. Who actually corrects people's posture, even an English bloke, in public like that? And I don't stand with a swagger. Actually, I don't stand masculine at all. Oh . . . and this would explain the voice in my ear, right in my ear it was, and the sense of threat. *You're standing wrong. You're standing like a girl.* Which I do. I wouldn't have been the first time. That time my brother got right in my face for the way I was walking down a staircase.

And it wouldn't be the last time I had no idea what someone was saying. So many moments like this, so many moments that were . . . concealed from me. The concealer helps me come out, to myself too. I feel naked and real with makeup on. I feel like I'm fake when it's off. Masculinity means performing that you're not performing. Erasing the erasure.

These jeans, these Japanese jeans (remember the jeans?)— they're so cool, I bought them in Norway before a lecture—*But why oh why are the pockets so small?* It's taken me six years to realize that they are women's jeans. I did it with that pair of boots in Oxford, I was nineteen. Fur-lined they were. Amazing. Where did they go? I was thinking Captain Kirk, just like everyone else wasn't. Now I know about me, I'm buying them deliberately, these things from the women's section.

It's a whole dissertation about objects, all this. How they're never "for" something or someone in particular, how they are never exhausted by how you appropriate them. How a pair of jeans is from a women's clothing shop in Bergen, Norway, and how it's not just for women. How people talk about "equipment" when they refer to male genitalia and how these "tools" are perceived as belonging to maleness or masculinity. It's funny, it's tragic, it's silly and frightening.

That's the thing about looking like a girl. You've entered a world of pretense, pretending—they call it *makeup.* Makeup, dress-up. But that doesn't mean you're totally pretending. And you really get what that quite misogynistic psychoanalyst, Jacques Lacan, says, in a voice that perhaps is a bit threatening, like that guy on the Victoria Line platform: *What constitutes pretense is that, in the end, you don't know whether it's pretense or not.*[1] That's the depth and the power of illusion—you can't tell in advance. And it's deeply part of what things are at all—a toothbrush, a black hole, a kimono. How they appear is never exactly what they are. But how they appear is how *they* appear. A toothbrush looks like a toothbrush. A kimono gives of all kinds of kimono data—it's not a sweater from Norway. Things are what they are, but never (quite) as they appear. Some people can't stand they ambiguity. They want to get rid of it, with violence.

It's funny, not quite seeing yourself for so long. You need reflections in your environment, ideas, people who can show you the right way. It took until quite recently, and a very kind and observant friend, to show me this about my gender. That was because while I don't identify with being male very much at all, I don't fancy boys. And while I have a strong gaydar, that strangely accurate mode in which you can see gender in others, I haven't been able to see it in myself . . . I was trying, in a state of agony pretty much, for ages to conform to being a straight man. And while I was doing so my being, my "body" or however you want to say it, was behaving otherwise.

"My body." I think when people say that, they often mean what OOO means when it talks about the parts of you that just are, the aspect that is what it is no matter what you make of it. I like my body. Now that I'm discovering more about what it is, I like it. There have been times when I've been very puzzled by it, afraid of it, or just surprised. It's surprising how, all through my life, I've entered a department store and headed for the women's clothing section, found something and bought it, just like that . . . just like that, without noticing that it's from the women's clothing section. There was one famous moment in 1990. I marched into a shop in the trendy Kensington Market, a place where all the ravers went to shop. I found something amazing. I tried it on in the shop. It looked great in the mirror. It was a small shop and there were I think three staff people, one man and two women. I bought it. Out I went, wearing it. It wasn't until a long time later that I realized it was a dress.

By *a long time later*, I mean not until 2020. I was having the deep and still ongoing experience of all my memories rearranging themselves, insights and laughter and tears, as I realized that I was non-binary. I was thinking about a band photo. I was in a band that my brother had started. They're still going. But in 1990 I was summarily kicked out, by my brother, who had said, "I think we all know why you can't be in this band." That phrase has haunted me for decades. Why did he put it that way?

Then I remembered the band photo. We had just seen it, a day before. In the photo, everyone was looking pretty "metal" and grim, but I was smiling ... surely that wasn't why I was being kicked out? It wasn't until last year that I realized that it was because I had been wearing the dress in that photo ... it really is quite mind-blowing, silly, funny, with a chaser of sadness. My brother had been starting to descend into schizophrenia, and had been acting very strangely. He had been acting very homophobic and had been getting into fights in pubs. Suddenly I realized what he had said and why he had said it.

Then there was the Strange Incident of the Agnes B Top. I was in New York City, doing my first job as a visiting assistant professor at NYU. My girlfriend was very queer positive but she was very worried about this top. I had marched into Agnes B and bought it because it looked amazing (you can guess what's coming next). It was black, it was tight, a bit short in the arms, but never mind, it's awesome, went my thinking. Like these jeans I bought in Norway a few years ago. Teeny tiny pockets in the "wrong" place, but who cares, these are amazing, I'm totally wearing them, they really flatter my legs. Yeah, it's a thing. I very often buy women's clothes not even knowing they're women's clothes. The gendered interpretation of the clothes data sometimes just doesn't function.

There are these moments when I don't see gender at all, and that incident in the shop and the band photo was one of them.

Earlier, I had walked into the women's shoe section in the gray 80s mall in Oxford and bought a pair of boots. I didn't realize they were women's boots. They just looked amazing. I was teased mercilessly, again without realizing at all ... it's funny how you can have such a gigantic blind spot. But you can.

In the introduction I told the story of how at Princeton a few years later, I was kissing my girlfriend in a restaurant. The manager came out and said, "We can't serve your kind in here ... get out." That's exactly what she said. We left with our heads spinning trying to figure out what had happened. I had very long hair and she had mistaken me for a girl! Something that had happened on a plane a few months before—"I'm afraid you'll have to sit up front Ma'am," said the attendant, and to this day I'm not sure why he was afraid he was upgrading me to first class.

I'm being stalked as I write this. I look ambiguous. I was walking down the street a few weeks ago, carrying a parasol because it was very sunny. A parasol, not an umbrella. Yes, I got funny looks from men at work. I've installed a CCTV camera above my front door. The stalking has subsided. I haven't yet activated the camera. But I might have. It's a dance, life is. A dance of revealing and concealing.

9

Cowboy Costume

So I ended up working in Texas. It sounds like a joke, and it might be. Most of my life has been lived by accident. But when I was very young I refused to go anywhere without wearing my cowboy outfit. In particular, I refused to go to preschool or what they call playgroup in the UK, without wearing my tasseled suede jacket and my tiny ten-gallon hat and my fake revolver with the white plastic handle.

For quite a lot of my childhood I was that cowboy, or Spiderman. Spiderman was great because he was an ordinary boy in a costume, who just happened to have special powers. I think a lot about exhibitionism. My friends who say they're introverts (and myself) strike me as exhibitionists who are a bit phobic (or a lot phobic) about that aspect of themselves. You get a lot of funny reactions from doing things that are seen as weird, such as reading in public. Eventually you internalize them, yet you yearn to do those things. You start to feel safe under a spotlight or when there's a camera going and the green light is on.

What was great about that cowboy costume? It wasn't me. It didn't express me. It portrayed something without me getting involved.

What's so great about Texas? Maybe nothing. California always struck me as having a definite plan. It's not so clear in Texas. Not at all. The streets here are worse than they are in Beirut, I know, I've been. But there's something here.

Why I loved California came down to stamps. In a *Star Trek* way, Californians are superior to any European because they don't just empathize or sympathize with your enjoyment, they appreciate it. They can see what it would be like. The very first day I showed up there to live, I asked for stamps at my local grocery store. The clerk was so appreciative of my desire for stamps, he treated it as if it were a particular form of sexual pleasure. "No, he didn't have any stamps today, but soon, maybe in three days, I would get my stamps. Stamp pleasure is coming. Don't worry Tim. You'll get your stamp pleasure."

It was then that I realized *Wow, California really is an advanced civilization and I can learn from this place.*

But Texans are even more that way. Some of them are. Some of them are more that way, then they react to it, and they become terribly violent. When a Texan agrees with you, they will ventriloquize what you just said, in an uncannily emotionally accurate way. That's why there's some homophobia in Texas. They think valuin' gay people means becomin' them, because they are done with appreciatin'. They are about becomin'.

Which brings me to my cowboy costume. Couldn't go to playgroup or pre-school or whatever it's called without it. Now I wear makeup and live in Texas. It's the same thing. Some Texan trucks are so outfitted with spurs and leather that that machismo turns into drag. The first fake women's clothing I wore really was that tasseled suede jacket to preschool. Those high heeled boots.

So before we get into specifics, and there are plenty of them, let's just pause to note how seduction, at least how I try it, is always about failure, failing to coincide with who they think I am, including myself. How seducing always means you were already seduced-by. How all the guns are always silver cap guns with no harmin' potential at all. How the cowboy is the flaneur of the desert, a-starin' down the horror of modern life with the same dandified vibe as a Baudelaire or a James Bond, only with a handlebar mustache and an engraved silver harmonica.

How coming out of a Texan's mouth, anti-racism and anti-patriarchy sure would sound good to the whole world. Of course, that's not happening right now. What's happening is the dark side of the cowboy, who breaks the law in order to enforce it. Right now, the Texas government has empowered its citizens to be anti-abortion vigilantes, in a way that makes this empowerment hard to challenge, because it is literally outside the law.

I was enjoying the Texan patois a few paragraphs ago. Let's go back there, I didn't just move to the US of A, I done moved to the western US of A and I done lived here more than half my life. Has a way of rubbin' off on ya. A good way. There's a good thing out here as well as a bad thing, maybe the same way as how things relate to the geomantic qualities of the indigenous cultures of Australia, I don't really know. But there's a cobalt blue and a sandy dark red I never done seen before.

America does everything good and bad by seduction. Churchill was a famous asshole, who said a lot of true things. And one true thing he said was something like, "Americans always do the right thing—having tried everything else first." And that's because they do stuff by feel here. It's aggravating. But when they get down to it, they really do it.

If I sound right now like the fake cowboy narrator of *The Big Lebowski*, and all cowboys are fake, aka "dudes," well, that's deliberate. Because I reckon somethin' those fancy east- and west-coasters don't understand is, you gots to fall in love with stuff to really do it. Texans who may hold all kinds of strange hateful views about brown and black people but Texans cook the best food I've ever eaten in America, because they become brown and black people in the kitchen. It's true. Californians have the great "produce" and New Yorkers have the great ideas about what to do with it, but Texans actually fall in love with it and do it.

And what is a cowboy but a flaneur of the desert, a dandy in spurs and heels? Someone who's aping being a posh rich guy while having nothing at all and caring nothing for rich guy things. As opposed to trying to be liked by the posh rich guys by making a pile o' golden toilets. That sounds like a loser's game to me. When in the film *Casino Royale* Vesper says that James Bond wears his amazing suit "with such disdain," because he didn't come from money—well, she's on the money.[1]

The left had better get a whole lot more seductive or some coke boy from Queens fakin' being a mafia Don from New Joisey is going to be in charge forever, psychologically speakin'. And the only way to do that as far as I can tell is, start to insist on more pleasure, of a non-European kind. Like how Texan food is so much more edible than any of the shit I ate elsewhere in this godforsaken land.

Cowboy: it doesn't mean a boy fused with a cow, does it? It means a boy who is really adept at manipulating cows. A subject adept in manipulating objects. An adept slave owner.

This going-beyond-law-to-enforce-it thing is happening in the flare ups of fascism taking place particularly in the Anglo world, "Anglo" as we call white people "down here" in extremely multiracial Houston. It's as if the victors of the Second World War have obsessive compulsive disorder and are double and triple checking whether they should've actually been like Germany and Japan. It's as if they don't believe what they proclaimed in that war—surprise surprise.

I just spoke of Texas law enjoining vigilantism against abortion. But in general, the assault on abortion US-wide is a vigilante action. What the Supreme Court did in 2022, striking down *Roe v. Wade*, blatantly violates precedent in the name of naked male domination of the world in the shape of women's bodies. Actual conservatism would be about conserving the power of precedents, and indeed, actually protecting actual life. But now the right has to resort to the shock tactics of the French Revolution and its mythological being, the sovereign subject versus all the objects. Versus the stuff of life, which is accidental, mutated, broken . . . aborted. A genuine care for life would imply care for its intrinsically broken, erroneous qualities.

Now imagine a West Texas desert, a fence post, the late afternoon heat. A cowboy leans back against the post, pulling his

Stetson down to cover his eyes a little. The PSSST! of his cola bottle sounds like Aaron Copland's *Fanfare for the Common Man* reduced to one burst of fizz. Fade to black. *This is an ad,* you remember, you got caught up in the sound of crickets and birds and that orange, orange sun. And the rich Texan accent sounds around you in the darkness of the cinema:

> Life, a rare form o' chemistry. The fact that the accident called life can happen means we live in a universe where "stuff" is not inert or dead. Mechanical causation would just grind the world down to powder, but there's a little corner of it called life, keeps reversing time. Life implies we live in a universe where *genuinely new things* are happenin'.
>
> Another name for that is *future.*
>
> Another name for that is *error.*
>
> Another name for that is *abortion.*

10

Battersea Power Station

A gigantic pig, lying on its back. A gigantic modernist hulk. An abandoned power station in the London borough of Battersea.

A huge balloon in the form of a pig floats over Battersea Power Station. The balloon pig floats free of its moorings and ends up near to Heathrow airport, stopping flights for a while.

It's 1977. Pink Floyd was about to release the album *Animals* and the cover art, by Hipgnosis, had got out of hand. The huge inflatable pig floating above Battersea Power Station had come loose and was drifting towards Heathrow airport, which had to be shut down for a while. Deeply symbolic of that whole album, that era with its strikes and its punk and its almost-socialism and my parents' marriage breaking down. Broken, everything is broken.

Like I say, when I talk to people who have never been to London, I tell them that I was born on the cover of *Animals*. It's roughly true. I grew up next to exactly the same railway tracks, a few miles southwest. In a larger sense, I grew up in a post-industrial landscape. The gigantic pig is Battersea Power Station, decommissioned before I was born. If you travel overground, not like how I went to school but from Waterloo Station to Wimbledon, you will go past Battersea Power Station. Now it's swathed in luxury flats. I hate them. Where's my broken, dirty power station? I used to visit the Tate Gallery (now the Tate Britain) almost every weekend of my teenage years. I was so used to it, I was only smelling it for a while—the pictures had disappeared and what was left was a spacious, dusty smell. I loved it. I connect that smell not with the fancy art in there, but with Battersea Power Station, which is opposite the Tate Britain. I wasn't surprised they chose another power station nearby to be the Tate Modern.

William Blake lived nearby, in Lambeth.

No one has been able to figure out what to do with Battersea Power Station. Even the luxury flats that now populate it don't look like they've absorbed its Battersea Power Station-ness totally. I love that. No object can be totally appropriated by another, says OOO. I love that Battersea Power Station is broken and empty and vast. It's literally post-industrial. That whole area of Southeast London, I wonder whether anyone will ever run a Tube line through it. It's where drum and bass started. That melancholic, siren sound. That elegiac, pastoral feeling but with abandoned factories and railway lines with horsetails growing in the sidings. Horsetails are really, really ancient. Dinosaur-era plants. The strangely fertile sidings, made so by sulfur emissions from the trains. Councils making allotments for people to grow vegetables by the side of the rail tracks. Me living right on the very edge of West London on one side of those tracks, gigantically wide, wider even than the Thames.

Battersea Power Station is not from the 1930s. Battersea Power Station is from the future. It goes on without us.

When British Petroleum started to sponsor the Tate Britain, my favorite smell was gone. There's a word for that beautiful smell, it's a beautiful word: *petrichor*. The smell of dust after rain for example. Or the damp concrete smell of brutalist architecture. I love it. Like the National Theatre on the South Bank in between the power station and the Tate Modern . . . the one that looks like Alien's body, this rusty-looking exoskeleton of concrete and smoked glass.

Every time I'm on a train to Waterloo or Victoria, I try to see Battersea Power Station. Like I say, there have never been enough underground trains through this area of London, which I'm sure many would agree is considered the most abject in the imaginations of Londoners: Lambeth, where William Blake lived. The East End has a certain underworld glamour. Northwest London is where genuine posh people live. Southwest London is where fake posh people live. Northeast London is Arsenal and Tottenham. But what, oh what is Southeast London? There's a gigantic graveyard near a place called Earlsfield where my grandfather is buried. We never went there. My mum's family is four generations of atheists and mostly very left wing and we didn't really think we needed to visit a grave.

I'm proud that I grew up on the very edge of Southeast London.

We're standing before that secret door again. The Afrofuturist part of me (I love Afrofuturism) believes that there must be many portals in Southeast London.

Just before 1977, the band Throbbing Gristle invented what was eventually called Industrial Music. Some of them had staged an exhibition at the Tate Gallery called *Pornography*. It caused a huge scandal. Cosey Fanni Tutti's photographs of her naked body ... provocative, powerful and unashamed, daring the viewer to react. I associate those photographs with Battersea Power Station.

Meanwhile, back in an earlier phase of agricultural civilization ...

We have the biggest and most accurate clock in the world, therefore we are now your rulers. Now make a physical model of it, by cutting this stone out of this Welsh mountain and dragging it two hundred miles. We will then sacrifice you in the middle. We are the druids.

Welcome to Stonehenge.

The fact that Stonehenge is on an army firing range is not an accident. The fact that it is now monetized and policed by British Heritage, created by Margaret Thatcher, to keep the hippies out, is not contrary to its purpose. In a way, she is a much more accurate user of Stonehenge than Hawkwind. It was always a part of British Heritage, metaphorically speaking. The druids were always fake druids, like the ones who perform a ritual there to this day. It was always on a firing range where ordinary people went to die.

I'm bringing Stonehenge and Battersea Power Station together because, in their very different ways, they're "power stations," and they're structures that aren't being "used" the way they used to be. They have a stark weirdness to them like the monolith in *2001: A Space Odyssey*. They tell us something true about things in general: things in general are never exhausted by what a particular group of humans does with them. Being a Styrofoam cup between my lips, full of coffee, is only part of the story. Most of the time, that cup is a crumpled mess in a landfill somewhere.

Defunct power has a certain charm—it can't hurt you anymore. People marvel at the pyramids rather than cowering in terror. And you're always living in amongst the broken bits of the past. That's partly what "the present" really means. Just a whole lot of junk. Think about the oxygen you're breathing. It's from bacterial poop. It's their pollution. It's maybe the first colossal ecological disaster on Earth. It nearly destroyed them, except for the ones that were able to hide, for example by having other single-celled organisms accidentally swallow them. That oxygen event is an explosion that is still happening. The Big Bang is an explosion that is still happening. You and the stuff you can see around you is just the current state of the wavefront.

I like to think that we live within a series of nested, concentric explosions.

My face is some kind of map of everything that happened to my face. When I was nineteen, I had terrible, terrible acne. I was a guinea pig for the drug they call Accutane in the USA. I can still see the scars. My face, my exploding face. An explosion theory of time is a good way of understanding trauma. We can be triggered, because trauma means *that thing is still happening.* There's no mystery to being triggered. There's nothing wrong with you if it happens. It happens to me, a lot. It's like burning your skin. You may not see the burn but it's still spreading in your finger under the surface. In a way, the present moment is just exactly all the traumas we haven't yet processed. All the stuff that's still weighing us down.

In a way, the present is just the past. Everything is kind of Stonehenge or Battersea Power Station. That lump of green soap I've had for a year next to my bath.

I don't believe very much in the concept we call "present." I'm a meditator, but I don't think that's about "being here now." Here and now are overrated, jumped-up bits of measurement. You can cut that cloth to any length you want, depending on what you want to do. You're an electron? For you the present means nanoseconds. You're an imperial army? For you the present means how long it takes to sail around the Cape of Good Hope and colonize the "spice islands." The present time of slavery isn't some dot on a Wikipedia line. The time of slavery is still happening, exploding all around us: it's called the United States of America.

I'm not really allowed to say that. Two sentences ago I just broke a new law, a new Texan law, by mentioning structural racism. The right here are stuck, yelling stuff like "America has no shadow side, no unconscious! Don't ever mention it in public! If you do, you should be severely punished." It's a mirror image of their fantasy that there is a repressive "cancel culture" shutting the mouths of freedom-loving people. But as we know, freedom of speech is not the same thing as endorsing saying terrible things to people.

Stinking away in the background here is the reactionary idea that humans really do want to rape and murder, and they must be physically stopped from so doing. How about the impulses embedded in the spectacle of a police officer strangling a Black man to death for the crime of being Black in public?

But this repression idea is exactly what Freud wasn't about. "Unconscious" means *You as a person actually don't want to do that*. For me, repression is about *increasing* pleasure. Committing a murder means you become alienated from your world. So a murderous society that beats you to death for existing hasn't mastered murder. I love this idea by the philosopher Jacqueline Rose:

> It is a central tenet of psychoanalysis that if we can tolerate what is most disorienting—disillusioning—about our own unconscious, we are less likely to act on it, less inclined to strike out in a desperate attempt to assign the horrors of the world to someone, or somewhere, else. It is not ... the impulse that is dangerous, but the ruthlessness of our attempts to be rid of it.[1]

Mike drop. Now, where was I? Ah yes, the present moment.

I don't believe in the present—well, not much anyway. But I do believe in the future, as well as the past. Not in some dot-version of the future either. That's also just a measurement. Don't confuse things with how you measure them. I know it's very tricky with regard to time. Think of it this way. The future you can predict depends on a future that might be very different from now. That's why you need to make a prediction. If it was the same, then you wouldn't need to worry. The actual future, what I sometimes call the *future future*, is in fact the very possibility that things can be different at all.

And in that sense Battersea Power Station and Stonehenge are the future, as well as the past. What is a stone circle? What should we "do" with Avebury now? What do stone circles really mean? It's like looking at a poem. In a way the poem is just the past—a whole lot of decisions, deliberate and not, to put a rhyme here, a metaphor there . . . But what does this poem mean? We don't know . . . yet. We know it's not totally meaningless. You can read this sentence. You just don't know exactly what it will have meant to you three weeks from now. The meaning, it's sort of there and not there, like a ghost.

Old, vast broken things like Battersea Power Station put us in touch with this ghostly quality that haunts things. Things are haunted by their future. Meaning is the future of this sentence. It's not exactly "in" the sentence, but it's not exactly "not in" it either. It sort of haunts the sentence. The future haunts the past. Things can be different. You never know how the past will turn out.

What are all those luxury flats doing, cladding my favorite building? Perhaps they're not just obscuring the past. Perhaps they're trying to cover up the future. Perhaps that's what I actually don't like about them. It's not that they are getting in the way of something more authentic underneath. It's that they're preventing a future where luxury flats are no more from coming into view.

In a strange and wonderful way, Battersea Power Station is the gigantic future, only just hidden behind those flats. It's like what the revolutionary French political art group, the Situationists, wrote on the streets of Paris in 1968: *Beneath the street, the beach.*

There is always an excess in things, an excess we can't point to or appropriate. It's called the future. This future is nowhere to be found outside of things themselves. Time is a kind of energy or liquid that things emit. I love this title of a piece of orchestral music by Toru Takemitsu: *From Me Flows What You Call Time.* I can imagine Avebury Ring and Battersea Power Station saying that.

Or maybe less pretentiously, the excess in things is like what the lead guitarist says about the druids in the infamously funny "Stonehenge" scene in the rock mockumentary, *This Is Spinal Tap*: "No one knows who they were ... or what they were doing ... but their legacy remains ... hewn into the living rock of Stonehenge ..."[2] Even they didn't know what they were doing, not completely. Do I know what I'm doing, writing this? Can I anticipate every reaction to it? Can I bake that into this book? Wouldn't be much of a book if I could. In fact, if I really could do that, the weight of the past—including all the predictions I've just made—would be totally paralyzing. Nothing at all could happen.

Things can happen because they are mysterious. Battersea Power Station happens without us. Long may it continue.

11

Sound File

Today it's October 29, 2020. Today my friend Amy posted a sound file she had made on Facebook. It's a WAV file, one of the most accurate kinds of sound file. It's a few minutes long. It's very special. It's a gift.

Amy is a sound artist. It's hard to describe some kinds of sound. If I tell you that in part this file contains the sound of some things Amy heard in a very remote part of Finland, you will be none the wiser. If I tell you that it's soft and slow and crackly and crunchy, you might get a feel for its texture, but you won't know everything. Maybe I can come up with a word like *bang*. I'm good at coming up with words. But if this kind of word is really accurate, it will be the sound itself and you won't know what it is either! *Describing things* and *being things* are actually on a spectrum. *Describing things* and *causing* things are also on a *spectrum*. OOO doesn't think that words like "cause" are big and grown up and real and strong while words like "illustrate" are flimsy and feminine and ineffectual. OOO believes that the aesthetic dimension, where things are accessed, paraphrased, illustrated—*translated* to use Graham Harman's beautifully succinct word—is the causal dimension.

These sentences are translations of Amy's sound file. Amy's sound file is a translation of somewhere in Finland. To translate is always to make some kind of difference—in short, to effect something, to have an effect . . . to *cause* something. Once you get used to it, this is a really wonderful way of thinking. It saves a lot of energy because you aren't making spurious distinctions any more between cause and effect and seeing or smelling or writing a poem about or recording.

The way we imagine "cause and effect" is from before 1750, from before Hume blew up the idea that you can directly see causes and their effects. Modern science swears by Hume. It looks at patterns in data. It doesn't try to look under the hood at the things themselves. It can only measure data. Those measurements are biological, or physical or what have you accountings of data, not things themselves.

Hume argued very successfully that you can't ever know for absolute sure that this billiard ball is going to hit that billiard ball, the millionth time you roll this ball towards that ball. What does it mean? It means you simply can't see the one ball as the cause of the other ball rolling. You just can't. All you've got are data, "things that are given" (English for the Greek *data*). Or to put it in the words of Roger Waters, in his song "Breathe," "All you touch and all you see / Is all your life will ever be." Right. And it's all a frog's life will ever be. And it's all a stick's life will ever be. And it's all a wave's life will ever be. And it's all a galaxy's life will ever be.

I bet that when you try to imagine "cause and effect" you visualize something like those balls, or maybe cog wheels, churning away underneath appearances. Clocks are so pre-1750. Cause and effect don't work like that. Cause and effect are not underneath. They're in front. Finding cause and effect is like music appreciation. When I said this to a room full of a thousand engineers in Singapore, they tried really hard to kill me for three days. I'm not sure physicists would be so prejudiced.

Quantum theory tells us that the universe is fundamentally not mechanical. It's not a clock. And this in turns means that the idea that there are things that are "alive" and things that are not is really, really overdue for the wastebasket. I don't like that distinction, between animate and inanimate. It's Aristotelian, it's not OOO. OOO pretty much holds that things are alive. Lively, at least. I think alive, in many senses of the word—trembling, quivering, vibrating. The most basic things in our universe—quanta such as electrons or photons—are shimmering all the time. They're moving without being pushed. I find this an incredibly moving and hopeful thing. If things are moving, it means things can be different, all by themselves. New things can happen. Creativity is deeply woven into the very structure of reality itself.

The future is everywhere. But you can't see it. All you can see is the past. That's what OOO says. It makes me cry. It makes me feel relieved. The baddest, darkest, most cynical theory of how we're trapped and paralyzed can't be true, that's what this means. You know how, if you've ever taken a "theory" class in the humanities, arts, or architecture, you know how it's a kind of unspoken competition? A competition for who can say the most cynical thing. Whoever says that is the winner. *I'm the teacher because I say the most cynical things. You have no idea how paralyzed you really are. That idea you're suggesting, about how fucked up everything is, is nowhere near as fucked up as they really are. That makes me smarter than you. Now give me $5000 and a nice hotel room and a huge meal for telling you all that you're fucked.* (The teacher wasn't even teaching that week. They left for a talk on a jet plane.)

Since when did convincing everyone that we're totally paralyzed become a substitute for caring about poor suffering workers?

I mean this most sincerely. It's a real problem in my world. It's a problem that OOO is trying to fix. The way it tries is very interesting. It takes two competing theories of ideology and joins them together. Without OOO these theories are at war with one another. But really they are connected. You just have to adjust the way you see things. You just have to generate some respect for the stuff of life.

To see how the future is everywhere, you just have to look at a little thing. Some people say you can see the whole of the structure of the universe in a droplet of water, or one subatomic particle. The whole of the past. I think you can also find the future in that droplet.

It's like what William Blake said about a grain of sand. You can find the whole world in it. Utopia is everywhere. It means "no-place" and "good place" at the same time. If it's no place, how can it be good? If it's good, how can it not exist? But this is the whole thing. The no-place quality is exactly the good place quality. It's not that it is no place at all. It's no-hyphen-place. It's a place. But it's not a place you can point to. It's not something versus nothing. It's wavering, shimmering something-ness, it's a curtain wafting with nothingness. It's a cloud. It's like what Yoko said about rain on the back of the *Imagine* album: "Imagine the clouds dripping. Dig a hole in your garden to put them in."[1]

What has this got to do with music? Everything. That little thing could be the sound file. You never hear music on its own. You hear a sound file. You hear an MP3. You hear a clarinet. Music is a thing, and music is produced by things. You never just hear "music," you hear D-flat major, you hear plainsong, you hear a Bulgarian women's choir.

I come from what they call a musical family. One of my earliest musical memories is listening to my dad practicing his violin on a weekend morning. He was playing a series of chords that I later learned were fourths and fifths. Later, much later ... when I was in my early twenties, in fact ... I discovered that what he was practicing was the violin solo for "Larks' Tongues in Aspic Part I," an iconic song by the progressive rock band King Crimson from what many regard as their supreme album, *Larks' Tongues in Aspic*.[2] He wasn't credited on the album—he took a big fee instead. That violin solo is definitely an "object" the way I see it— it has its own autonomous life on that album and in the minds of anyone who loves that album. I'm wearing my *Larks' Tongues in Aspic* t-shirt right now. It's an alchemical sun-and-moon figure.

Violins. There were lots of them, because both my parents were concert violinists. I decided I needed to be a violinist too, aged five. An instrument, if you haven't played one, is its own kind of entity. Learning to play one, you realize that instruments of all kinds—a fork, a tennis racket, a computer—aren't just extensions of your body. At least they aren't simply ways of making what your body already does more efficient or effective. They extend them a way an ill-fitting pair of shoes might, or a car that you have to trick into finding second gear. *You extend yourself into them.* It's not the other way around. You learn what violins like. They don't like it too cold. They don't like humidity but they really don't like when it's dry. They like keys with a few flats in them—not too many. Sharps sound, well, sharp, acidic, sour.

Violins don't like "equal temperament," the tuning mode popularized first by Bach and now hard-wired into every computer on the planet. Equal temperament is a way to blend lots of different key signatures together on a keyboard such as a piano. Equal temperament creates a way of telling a story about lots of human emotions in a way that knits all those emotions together in a seamless way. "First I was feeling angry, then I was frustrated—after that there was a burst of fear and then I felt a sense of tremendous calm." The "I" in that sentence seems to underlie all the feelings. It's like looking at a sepia watercolor painting. All the trees and the water and the mountains are made of the same stuff. It's reliable. It can be boring. It's definitely using your instrument as an extension of your human being-ness.

Have you ever heard a piece of music composed using "just intonation"? It's when you tune the instrument to whole-number ratios. If you've been in a bath of equal temperament all your life, it's a revelation. It's like you've spent all your life eating hamburger … then someone offers you a slice of lemon. It's sharp, sour, it makes you salivate. It's not "pleasant" like you understand it. But it weirdly sort of is. Musical instruments are constantly trying to get out from under the iron yoke of equal temperament.

There was a shop near me called Cloud 7 when I was under ten years old. After that, it was the basement of the HMV shop in Oxford Street that did it for me. I would go in there just to hold the records. I couldn't afford them, mostly. But it was amazing to wonder what they might sound like, trying to figure them out from their sleeves, which is like trying to figure out what someone is saying from the way they dress. Which can be possible … Looking at these silent records, it was as if I was hearing them, but in a different way. I spent hours in those shops, fingering my way through Genesis and Yes albums for example (Cloud 7) and avant-garde classical music such as Stockhausen (the HMV shop). I was keeping my taste secret from my dad. Secret from myself, even, given that I hardly bought anything. It took me months to save up enough money and courage to by my first Stockhausen record. Buying it was like committing a crime.

The outer moons of Saturn. That's where music teleports me, especially if I'm the one playing it. It's one reason why I've avoided trying to do it for a job. It's very hard to write a report or clean the floor if you're on the outer moons of Saturn. It's very hard to make yourself understood. If I play a musical chord at 5pm, I might still be at it at 5am.

My body, that's what the outer moons of Saturn are, really. Music puts me in my body, and when my body is doing the thing called dancing, it's very happy. And even when I'm not moving my body, music makes me feel its gravitational pull. Hence those outer moons.

Music is a very good example of a being that shows me how I am definitely not the master of my universe. Not even close. Not even the security guard or the janitor. Music is evidence that life goes on without me.

I get overwhelmed by the potential of music. I love it when I'm in the mood. "Can You Feel It"—it's a thing you say at a rave and it's the title of a tune you might have played at one, in 1988, a tune made by Mr. Fingers.[3] The "it" is never directly specified but you know what it is. It's a feeling of utopia, a feeling of immense pleasure, and perhaps most of all the feeling of being in a crowd, not just a crowd, a collective, a group. A feeling of being on a mission, even if you don't have one very carefully spelled out. This *Can you feel it?* is something I associate very strongly with the nonverbal pull of music. It's something on the tip of your tongue. It's the future.

It was this future that a single stroke of my brother's stick or brush on a single drum could open up for me. People can hit drums and they do things to you. I once studied with some Native American women shamans. They played all kinds of rhythms for us. We immediately stated what they were evoking, completely accurately. "Universal support" is the rhythm I remember best, a steady rhythm, light and not fast, but not too slow. I remember from twenty-five years ago like it's today. Music does that to me.

12

The Chicken

So there's this guy. He's paranoid that he's being persecuted by a giant chicken. He checks in to an asylum. After a few months of therapy there, he's feeling a lot better. He doesn't believe in the chicken anymore, and the head psychiatrist discharges him with a clean bill of health.

But a few weeks later, the guy returns to the asylum. He's shaking, sweating, he's white as a sheet. He bursts into the head psychiatrist's office without knocking. The psychiatrist looks up from his work. "Oh—it's you! What on earth is the matter? You seemed totally cured a few weeks ago."

"The chicken! The chicken!" The guy can hardly get the words out.

"But Septimus! My dear Septimus!" says the psychiatrist, kindly and firmly. The guy's name is Septimus and, most of the time, he lives in a novel by Virginia Woolf. He has severe PTSD.

"I know." Septimus is gasping for air, he's been running, presumably from the chicken.

"So my dear fellow, why are you here? You know there isn't a chicken!"

"Yeah—but try telling that to the chicken."

I love that joke. I first heard Slavoj Žižek tell that joke. I'm not sure where. But I love it for the reasons why he told it. Very often in life, it's not good enough to convince ourselves and others that some course of action is right or not, or what have you. Think about global warming. We know the truth, we know what to do. But we're not doing it.

You have to convince the chicken.

This is a chapter about the chicken, or, as you may have guessed, the unconscious mind. The part of "you" that goes on without you. Now that's an OOO object if ever there was one. A gigantic chicken. A chicken that doesn't live "in" individual people, but instead in the way you walk down the street, mow the lawn, ignore white supremacy. The stuff of life indeed.

I'm talking about the brain. The brain is the chicken. Chicken brain.

I spend most of my time writing in such a way as to convince the chicken. Let's just say "stupid people" shall we, and get it over with. I'll say it so you don't have to. We're all stupid at some level. Once you've learned something, it gets hardwired. Did you know that the conscious mind processes about fifty bits of information per second? A bit is something like a one or a zero. On or off. Your unconscious mind processes twenty million bits per second.

Twenty million bits. So that when you're driving, you don't have to think. There's a wonderful clip from a show by neuroscientist David Eagleman. It's called *The Brain*, and the clip (easy to find) is about a boy who can stack cups faster than anyone else in the world.[1] It's a thing American kids do at school. You make a tower of cups and then you un-make it, a few different ways. He can do the whole routine in a couple of seconds. When wired up, the boy's brain shows precisely no activity at all. That's right. That's why we talk about muscle memory. It's real. David Eagleman's brain, on the other hand, was lighting up like a fireworks display as he tried to stack those cups. To this extent, thinking is the symptom of a malfunction, and may itself be a kind of malfunctioning.

It's not so hard to convince people who are ready to think. Ready to let their world go a bit wrong, look funny, be challenged. Ready to be surprised. The trick is, how do you convince people who can't be persuaded like that? It took years and years for Indian Buddhists to convert Tibetans. The Tibetans were rugged resistant cowboys. Legend has it that every night the demons tore down the Buddhists' temples, which is legend speak for "their brains simply rejected the information." Then along came Padmasambhava, who has been considered a great holy man in Tibet since then. He didn't try to convince people. He just blew their minds. He did miracles. He spoke to the chicken. He changed people's brains.

Come to think of it, your brain kind of is a nice plump chicken sized thing, all snug in its egg-like skull nest.

I've always been very interested in brains. Now I'm even more interested. Brains are one heck of an amazing object, perhaps the most complex in the known universe. Fortunately, they are malleable: the phenomenon of "neuroplasticity," which means you can change your brain, was validated by hooking up Mingyur Rinpoche, my meditation teacher Tsoknyi's brother, to some electrodes in 2002. You ought to be able to change your brain. That's how you can get over phobias and learn a new skill. But for ages we white Western people thought that brains were totally set in stone once you reached adulthood.

This says a lot about what we think about objects in general. We think that they are unchanging lumps, unchanging until something hits them. But what if they were squirming around all by themselves? "There's a killer on the road, his brain is squirmin' like a toad" (The Doors).[2] That's what it can feel like sometimes. Your brain runs on drugs called neurotransmitters. That's what they do—they transmit. Things move. Neurons fire in cascades or showers, that's how we talk about them. When you look at the EEG of David Eagleman stacking cups, his brain activity looks like a chicken squirming in a very cramped disco. We think objects are static. This is a big mistake, a mistake with massive ideological consequences. We've been giving up on the possibility that "adults" can play, in essence. "Adult" is almost defined as a being who can't or shouldn't play. Well maybe they could play a bit of golf. But they shouldn't fool around too much ... that would be crazy.

This is very depressing. No wonder people are discovering that taking low doses of psilocybin is really good for you. It's a chemical that makes your brain play, on a very deep level. It makes your brain squirm and squiggle about. Heaven knows whether what you "see" when you're tripping is "true" or not. The main point is, your brain got some wiggle room. Psilocybin is used to treat depression, which is that feeling of total solidity, no exit, hopelessness. The reason, the fundamental reason, why this is a terrible thought is, *it is not true*. You need a lot of processing power to sustain it, because that thought is untrue. Like patriarchy and white supremacy, it's kind of just some sort of congealed load of shit.

High level Buddhist meditation says, *Reality is just like the reflections in a crystal ball. Just "be" the ball for a while. Don't worry about the reflections.* It's such a relief—it gets really simple the higher up you go, which is interesting, as if, like all other religions, the "lower" stuff was just to keep peasants in line. In truth, the highest explanation of so-called "emptiness" (the fact that things are beyond concept), is that it's a feeling. That's why it's represented and expressed by the Sanskrit syllable AH, which is the sound we make when we sigh with relief. Ah, thank goodness! There's some wiggle room!

But isn't the crystal ball really your brain, your lovely biological brain, that inheritance of your place in evolution in a biosphere? Isn't that what we're actually alienated from, not some divine being in the sky, but our biological being? I find that telling myself "Just be your brain" when I meditate is really soothing, and easier on my mind than mystical stuff about crystal balls. I don't have this residual side effect of thinking that mind is good, matter is bad. We keep snapping back to some kind of Platonism, which is really nihilism: this physical world is just a bad photocopy of something more real called an Idea. What if it were the other way around, that your ideas (including your idea of yourself) were really just very narrow, reified, congealed patterns in your brain?

I think this is why psychoanalysis works. I was in analysis for twenty-five years. The best part isn't the ideas, who knows about them (the Oedipus complex and so on). The best part is the part academics who haven't actually been in analysis don't really appreciate and never tell you about: *free association*. You read a lot of stuff, often by Lacan—he had a lot of technical terms and seems like a bit of a know-it-all, which is attractive to intellectuals—about *object petit a, the subject supposed to know, the Big Other* and so on. I can talk this talk with the best of them. It has nothing to do with actual psychoanalytic therapy.

Free association: what a simple and brilliant idea. It's based on the assumption that your mind and brain are in motion. Movement is part of how they are. You just get stuck sometimes, that's all. So just let your mind wander, witnessed by your analyst, who has also been trained to free associate. At first I thought my analyst Bob was really intelligent—he is, but I mean I had all kinds of paranoid thoughts: "How come he can anticipate all my ideas, how come he's even faster than I am, always waiting for me around the corner I am dodging around so as to avoid him?" He wasn't. He was just really, really adept at free association. Your analyst is just this guy who is really good at that. That's what you learn. You might start thinking *Oh, this guy is really helping, he's more powerful than my dad or mum, he knows me better than me* ... But you shouldn't end up there. Where you land is, *Oh, this is just another guy who learned this amazing simple thing called free association. And I've just paid him over a hundred thousand dollars over the course of twenty-five years to find that out!* (I believe the right insertion here is LOL, although I'm not sure who is laughing or why, which probably deserves another LOL.)

Free association is a neurological lubricant, that's what I think. There's some kind of feedback between conscious thoughts and the actual hardware. That's why you do analysis. That's why you have "breakthroughs" and cathartic feelings. Because you're letting your "mind" float, and thereby allowing your brain to find new ways of creating patterns. Chickens need a massage sometimes.

Some facts take a lot of lubrication to discover. For instance, it took all those twenty-five years of my therapy to figure out that I have PTSD or post-traumatic stress disorder (I hope we all know that phrase by now). It was worth it. Obviously my PTSD is really intense otherwise it wouldn't have taken so long to discover. It's such an old condition for me that it has felt totally default.

PTSD is a kind of brain damage. You forget stuff, you blank it out, you act it out like a zombie, it's terrible. But unlike anxiety, it's not a symptom of existing as such. What I mean is PTSD is not chronic, although the acuteness may go on for decades! You can treat PTSD using EMDR, which involves the physical movement of your eyes. That's really interesting in itself. You can cure something supposedly about "your life" and your terrible story and so on, by just moving your eyes! You can heal some of it using MDMA, or *molly* or *ecstasy* as it's called. Vietnam vets are now allowed to take it, for this very reason: it works.

It's a brain thing. The MDMA floods your brain with serotonin (and other neurotransmitters), giving you a brief but very salutary and very physical (remember the brain is physical) glimpse of feeling sorted out, that you can learn from.

There's an idea that philosophers and scholars in general shouldn't do drugs because that would be the thinking equivalent of dosing yourself with steroids at the Olympics. Thought should be drug free, thinks white Western culture at large. But your brain runs on drugs. That's what a neurotransmitter is. That's why drugs work, for good and bad. When you have a headache, there's no point in figuring out how you got it, how you could change your behavior and so on to avoid it—I've heard many New Age people talk this way, it's very oppressive. When you have a headache, you take a pill.

How do you tell billions of brains, *Don't use fossil fuels. For god's sake stop burning petroleum.* Really, how do you do that? Like, right now. I'm all ears. We've got about ten years before it gets even worse outside.

In the case of reading this paragraph, your conscious mind is doing the work of understanding, but somehow the words I'm using have to talk to the chicken as well. So you have to talk in an oblique way. They say the truth cannot be pointed to directly, but only evoked. All the words are broken. In fact, if OOO is right, then this "truth" is about everything in the whole universe, because you can never point to something directly. You can only sneak up on things. You can't own them totally. You can never see all of them, either over time or all at once. You can never see all of them, even if you grind them into the finest powder.

Heidegger was once standing in a lecture theater. "How about this chalk?" he goes. "What do you think it is? Well science perhaps would say, let's find out what it's made of. So let's begin there. Let's snap it in half." With a clean click, Heidegger snaps the chalk. He holds both bits up to the students sitting in the lecture theater.[3]

"Oh—whoops," he goes. "Now we have two problems." (I'm paraphrasing.)

I often feel that I get paid to say the wrong thing in public. Heidegger said something "wrong"—look, this chalk has a permanent underworld no matter how much you pulverize it. Heidegger was pointing out the unconscious, which is always provocative even when it seems only to concern a bit of chalk.

There is one huge reason why I learned to say the wrong thing. One massive chicken called America. America is the id of Europe. It was where Europe outsourced all the slavery to, and it hasn't recovered. America is like a machine-learning algorithm: it screws up every which way until it gets it right. Europe is the programmer. America is the brain. Europe is the mind. America is the patterns laid down by Europe in its colonial capitalist phase. Europe had the idea of Eden. Then they had to go and create it for real. It's called colonialism.

America is a brain with PTSD.

America. In my opera I wrote: *Welcome to America: the greatest pile of Europe EVER.*[4] It's funny and it isn't funny. There are giant shoes by the side of the road here, houses made of thousands of beer cans in Houston, "the world's largest" whatever. But America itself is a pile. The idea of colonialism was to build up a gigantic pile of money, and then the automatic version started, the one called industrial capitalism. Marx calls it *primitive accumulation.* I don't think America a country quite yet, because of the slavery required to create that enormous pile of wealth. It's easy to make money when the workers are doing it for free.

So much about America is like the psychoanalytic id, not the ego, not the superego. Well, okay, superego: we have nuclear missiles and we go around telling people how to behave. But as you may know, the superego is a part of the id that got repurposed. And as you know, American foreign policy is quite, quite irrational. America is pure Harpo Marx, with some superego Groucho thrown in. Sure, some of us have nuclear tipped warheads and stupid ideas about god and white supremacy. But also, we have t-shirts, blues, funk, fast food, heavy metal, Black Lives Matter, #MeToo—we have things that billions of people love, because we're not really a country. They explode around Earth.

You can find the best as well as the worst of America, in a pile. Like Harpo Marx we can hardly speak; instead we squeeze old car horns and have weird not-quite-maniacal grins. America doesn't have a clue. Really. Just listen to Americans. They never sound like they're going to take over the world, not the regular ones anyway. And even the not-regular ones. "Chemical Ali," the right-hand man of Saddam Hussein in Iraq, said something amazing while the Americans were invading Baghdad. The TV anchor was saying "Americans now have control of Baghdad," whereupon Chemical Ali retorted, "Nonsense. American's can't even have control over themselves." Snap.

Everything is like this here. We have gigantic shops that are more like warehouses than shops—and so do you, because of us. My house, built in 1929, contains bits of the 1920s, 1930s, 1940s

... all jumbled without rhyme or reason. We've got coins, contactless cards, chip cards, credit cards without chips, gold under the bed, everything. The English language. It's not really a language, is it? It's just a pile of everyone else's words with a pile of various people's rules thrown in.

The ultimate American slogan is, *If it ain't broke, don't fix it.* The id: you as an "it," as a being despite your idea of that being. At this level you can't be "broke" because you never functioned. Everything is a kind of malfunction, a something thrown on a garbage pile.

A pile finds it hard to be coherent. We Americans are so ambiguous. So uncertain. Trump is keen on Village People's "YMCA." Perhaps it evokes the best fun he had without reference to his parents, dancing to that in New York's infamous Studio 54. Hitler wouldn't ever have had Black or gay music in the house, or Germany. I suddenly see that's one reason why people voted for a broken clown: because he is a broken clown. This is broken clown land. Racism forced Obama to look and act perfect, in a land made of funky broken beings. It was a tragedy. One false move and he was toast. Part of the racism against him has come in the form of violent outrage at his attempts not to make a single mistake. It's horrible.

Trying to persuade people here is like trying to persuade people in a dream. Sometimes, a lot of the time, no matter how loud you shout or how brilliant you are, people just won't listen. PR comes from here. PR is just a dirty word for art. Art is just a euphemism for PR. Freud's nephew Edward Bernays got suffragettes to hold cigarettes and call them torches of liberty, and a few weeks later millions and millions of women were smoking. Even he was amazed. Facebook quizzes harvest your data and suddenly, you don't feel like voting against Trump. Goebbels learned a lot from Freud's nephew, Bernays. We have therapy by the bucketload here. Jacques Derrida's deconstruction really took off. His wife was a psychoanalyst. Psychoanalysis and deconstruction are deeply related. Both allow you to find slippery, slidy, shadowy inconsistent things. Neither of those took off in the UK, not even now really, not with this enthusiasm.

I owe a lot to my mum, so much. When I was getting a clue in the early 1980s, mum was friends with Greenham Common women who were busy stopping Reagan's cruise missiles from turning Britain into what Orwell calls it in *1984*: Airstrip One.[5] Mum read *Spare Rib*. After being a violinist she became a violin teacher, then a social worker, then a manager of daycare centers for at-risk kids, then a consultant for daycare centers. She used to put people in jail for doing unspeakable things to children. Then she became a psychoanalyst. Mum often tells me that therapy hasn't even now really taken off in the UK as it has in the USA. Somehow people can see things here. Yet they are so blind. They can see it's a dream. They see bullshit so clearly. Yet they are also so easily taken in. It's hilarious and frightening.

And the whole world now sees how we suffer from it, because we don't get out much. That's great, because most people aren't thinking "We want to take over the world." Mostly we just want to clean the car and mow the lawn. And we don't even know why. We have no clue. None. And it's *better* than Europe to that extent. We don't have a clue because there's never been a king to give us one. "Reality" comes from the same word as "royalty." If you think this is weird, it is, but realize that two very prominent Marxist intellectuals would've agreed with me: Gramsci and Kojève.

What we need here is someone to show us a different way to dream. Just a few funny looks should do it, one or two photos, a tweet, some mélange of photos with text (memes as we now call them). After the election I was struck by a photo of Vice President Harris leading Biden onto the stage. It looks like the girl leading the old man by the hand in William Blake's painting for his poem "London," like the spirit of feminism leading the broken droid of patriarchy. It's a dream. You don't need much. Once you figure that out, you can do it. But before then it might feel like you need something really huge. Some geniuses came up with three words from the future: Black Lives Matter. Wouldn't that be great? Three words ignited the whole world when a police officer murdered George Floyd.

The Anglo left right now (in America and the UK, that is) is decidedly bad at PR. The Anglo left has shouting and a kind of "told you so" vibe. How's that been working out. Grab them by the psychic pussy.

It might not even be onerous. Americans don't even know how to sit. They fiddle and put their feet on the table. "You're standing wrong" was a thing I heard first as a poor stupid American. It's so uncomfortable to slouch. Chewing gum hurts after a while. We have no clue. Poor stupid Americans, weighed down with all their meaningless European crap in a huge pile, in their gestures, what they wear, the white supremacy, everything.

The way you succeed here is based on the id: you just keep going. You just don't stop. If you're still standing, you're the winner. It's how the slaves escaped. Survival mode. Don't look around. You just keep on keeping on and suddenly you're being flown around to say the word "hyperobject" and people believe you.

We are the most unsure people on Earth. I just want to check, is this a book? This is a book you're reading, right? The one I wrote? I wrote this, yeah? So I must be using a computer now, right? I'm just checking. Have you had a conversation with an American person like that? You're thinking of having one, right? Are you? I just want to make sure you're reading this.

And we have all these bits of past-ness here. Just an endless pile of them. Arriving from the fickle UK where last week's pop music is totally forgotten, I couldn't believe how America was an elephant's graveyard of hits from the past. Supermarkets resonate with A Flock of Seagulls, Bill Withers, Phil Collins, Cyndi Lauper and XTC, and that's just the 80s stuff that fifty-something me now remembers, because I live in America. But it's an elephant's graveyard of all kinds of stuff. Fahrenheit. Inches. *Griddle*: British people: when did you last use "griddle" in a sentence? 1840? *Skillet*: we say skillet every day here. The Boston accent is a relic of the early 1600s. Want to know how Shakespeare sounded? Park your car in Harvard Yard.

Piles of old stuff, piled high for no reason. So many chickens, so little time.

White people started America in order to pile wealth high without rhyme or reason. Karl Marx has a good term for this early phase of capitalism, which involves colonialism and slavery: primitive accumulation.

Old broken stuff. Slavery. The Electoral College: an arcane piece of slavery-era voting rules that still functions today, with predictably racist results. The Electoral College, invented so slaves could count as "three fifths of a person" and add to their owner's vote. Literally—I know it sounds crazy and horrible. This slavery artifact is why this has been happening, "this" being the terrible resurgence of fascism in America. Al Gore and Hillary Clinton would've been president if there hadn't been an Electoral College. No Bush. No 9/11. And therefore no Trump.

When I first started to return to the UK for holidays, I noticed everyone immediately mentioning the new computers they had just purchased. There was definitely an envy of "tech" and a feeling that America was a high-tech sort of a place. But all the high tech is deceptive. It's for automating the past. Just consider what an algorithm is. It's a recipe. Take an egg, put it in boiling water, wait four minutes, remove, tap the shell at the top and peel it off—you have a boiled egg, a pretty perfect one for the altitude and climate of my home town of Houston. Computer programs are recipes. They're literally based on the past. This can have dangerous and violent consequences. Facial recognition software is based on the geometry of white supremacy, the American eugenics movements of the early twentieth century from which Hitler learned a lot. Every time you use facial recognition, you are helping an AI to machine learn how to employ this geometry more and more effectively. That should make you nervous.

You know how talking to an AI online is really, really frustrating? It's really to do with the efficient way in which the AI mashes up the past. Like a moronic genie or that wish-granting fish in the fairy tale, it will do whatever it's been programmed to do, nothing more and nothing less. You can't reason with it. You just have to know the right word to say. A few years ago, you could subvert a lot of automation in a call to customer service by yelling the word "Agent!" at every opportunity. Then you might quickly get through to a human being. I think "they" have managed to sew up this loophole since then.

It's like having to talk to people in a dream, trying to get people to do stuff here. It's sometimes as if everyone is already a kind of AI, and you're trying to find the magic word, and you can't. I was being stalked because of my gender last year. When I called the police, their first question was, "Is a crime being committed?" I had to make myself not ask what I wanted to ask: "Do I need to be getting raped or murdered before you send someone out?" It's the American dream all right—but not that lovely aspirational one, more like a nightmare where however loud you shout, people can't hear you. It turns out the American dream is a stupid idiot version of a dream inside a dream, a dream idea that isn't real. Not that. Every year, the actual American dream makes this dream less and less attainable.

Everyone here is speaking in some kind of weird reversed speech, like the infamous Black Lodge in David Lynch's wonderful *Twin Peaks* series.[6] Like in the Black Lodge, you somehow just find yourself there, this weird dimension that is sort of like being inside a television set. You have no idea how everyone ended up here: there's a weird dwarf who looks and sounds like he was an MC in some seedy New Orleans lounge. There's a stage magician from Las Vegas. You reach for your cup of coffee and find that it has become a viscous, bitumen-like substance that hardly oozes out of your cup when you turn it upside down. That's what it's like here. "The American dream" is just a wishful thinking version of that . . . like wishing you were home inside a dream when you are actually lying in bed but you have no clue. As two of the main characters in Twin Peaks put it, "We live inside a dream." We are basically all idiots here. Our very way of understanding ourselves is a form of idiocy, sometimes charming, sometimes menacing, sometimes a bizarre overlap of both.

Thinking that you know why you're here might actually be very dangerous. The "manifest destiny" white supremacy pioneer Manhattan Project type vibe. The psychic and political place that Twin Peaks calls the White Lodge. In the end, that's the scary one. The Black Lodge is just full of lost idiots. Whose dream is this, anyway? Knowing exactly what you're doing isn't a way of rising above it, here. That knowingness is also part of the dream you're in.

The risk of fascism is very high in the USA, with all the broken bits of the past lying around. It starts with holding on to old bits of dream because you are scared of something. Fascism gives you something to hold on to, a bit of dream to hide in. This white skin, this swastika, it must have some meaning and value . . . fascism is like rooting around on a beach with a metal detector for bits of gold. And once people have become fascists, you can't persuade them. You can't persuade someone in a dream to put down a dream weapon. It's infuriating. Everyone on Earth now sees how infuriating it is to live here. Old bits of meaning, old "tweets" and "memes" live on and on here, before the internet. The internet just made this very American phenomenon more efficient and automated. You can't persuade people whose heads are stuffed full of fascist tweets, and it's for the same reason you can't kill a virus—it's not really alive. You just have to become immune to it. A fascist meme is definitely a virus—it's a bit of old code wrapped in another form that then you get seduced into retweeting. Being right doesn't work. You have to blow people's minds. You have to make them immune to the virus. The virus happens without you. But let's just put it this way. Until anti-racism and anti-patriarchy can sound Texan there's no way to get the world to love on the polar bears right?

There is something amazing about how the comedian Patton Oswalt talks about a thing called the KFC Famous Bowl.[7] The Famous Bowl is quite literally a bowl full of things that you like at a fried chicken place: mashed potato, strips of chicken, beans, corn . . . there's no form, it's almost as if you're invited to put your face in it and eat like a dog. It's the secret form of America, from a chicken joint. There's that chicken again.

America, it's not just an American problem. And I'm not just talking about American imperialism. I'm talking about American products. We love them. Jeans. T-Shirts. Saying "gonna" or "LOL" or "lit" or . . . As Oswalt makes clear in his bit on the bowls, apropos of talking to chickens, the KFC Famous Bowl isn't just America's favorite. *The whole world* wants the Famous Bowl more than anything else from KFC. This isn't Houston's problem alone. This problem is worldwide, this problem called America.

The problem called America makes a lot of broken things because it's made out of broken things, broken bits of Europe. We don't really know why we have things like lawns and columns on our houses. We don't really know what lawns or columns are . . . We don't really know what mustard is, so we broke mustard and made our own, at the start of the twentieth century. "American mustard" or "yellow mustard" is a case in point. If you look at the ingredients (no one does) it is actually a fascinating combination of mustard seed, turmeric and vinegar. But everyone assumes it's a lower-class, tasteless mustard that one should avoid. Especially Americans. They can't wait to get their hands on something with grains or something that sounds French and is creamy and brown. A lot of us still have issues with "English mustard" but that's mostly because English mustard is basically English wasabi—it's mustard cut with horseradish and it could blow your nose clean off. I like boiling potatoes, scraping them and sprinkling them with English mustard powder, then drizzling on some olive oil and roasting them. But, as they say, I digress.

If you look at the ingredients of American mustard you won't necessarily find all kinds of artificial colors and flavors, as you might expect—how else could those awful Americans have gotten it quite so yellow? What you will find is mustard seed, vinegar and turmeric, mostly. Turmeric—one of the middle-class "superfoods" of the moment, the one that people take in tablet form to help with their inflammation and to display good taste. You know where the most amount of turmeric is eaten, in the world? At any good old US baseball game, where people put strips of American mustard on their hot dogs. (They'll need it, because those frankfurters can be quite inflaming.)

I don't believe anyone in Europe could've thought to combine mustard and turmeric. It's a too-bizarre mashup of the middle ages and early capitalism, the period I like to call the spice race (which sounds like the space race, but in a Cockney accent, and was exactly like the space race for all kinds of reasons).[8] American mustard broke the codes, crossed the wires, because it didn't know any better.

A couple of years ago I thought I would give it a try after many years of self-imposed exile from this flavor. I liked it. I really liked it. Once I had gotten over my own snobbishness and Eurocentrism, I found American mustard to be a perfectly legit form of mustard, unique. Ranch dressing is another American working-class delicacy. A farmer invented it after World War II in the absence of vinaigrette. It's dill and cream and some other stuff, basically. It's quite delicious. There are plenty of American foods made out of broken stuff. African-American food is made of offcuts and internal organs because of slavery. And it's delicious. Gumbo, the creole style soup based on okra ("gumbo" is derived from West African words for okra) and filled with bits of catfish, oysters, shrimp and rice is absolutely one of the greatest soups on Earth, if you ask me. Fried oysters. Grilled catfish, a freshwater shark that if you get just right is incredibly succulent.

Broken things. America created jeans, which are basically broken trousers. They are often sold "distressed" as if they have been broken for you. A t-shirt is a broken shirt—someone cut the arms off. Some guy is fiddling with radar, and suddenly his chocolate melts in his pocket and he's invented the microwave. It's made out of mistakes. The Blues is profoundly broken, cosmically malfunctioning music that breaks the European harmonic rules with that blue note, and which breaks the idea that music has to go somewhere, with its amazing ratcheting back into its starting position and the amazing ironies and depths and passions that can build up through this ratcheting. Jazz—a huge term for a vast field of musics—breaks the idea of music as a product and spectacle to be witnessed in "polite" silence and to be played in roughly perfect faithfulness to the musical score. A great trumpet player plays perfectly in tune, but a genius trumpet player continuously breaks the sound, letting the mouthpiece and the horn malfunction.

Black Lives Matter is made out of broken bits of white supremacist criminal "justice" and the broken bodies of men, women and children killed by a structurally racist police force that is very much a revolving door for the KKK. Its global appeal is like the global appeal of all great American things. Its iconoclasm—breaking statues of a slaveowner and throwing it in the river for example—is a profoundly democratic form of creativity.

Dreams are made out of broken bits of the waking world that your mind mashes up while you're asleep, like the ingredients in that KFC Famous Bowl. Let's put it this way: dreams are made out of broken bits of the past. Like poems, like this book. And what's amazing is, sometimes when you put broken bits of the past together, they can become a landing pad for the future. Or a portal through which you might touch it. Or a crystal ball.

America is a broken country. Better, America isn't a country at all, and that's because of slavery. Whatever America is, it's best to think of it as a huge pile of shattered things that, if you put them together in certain ways, you can see the future, like in a crystal ball. Black Lives Matter. #MeToo. The concept of non-binary gender. These are American exports, like t-shirts and jazz and Kentucky Fried Chicken. There's a reason why they arose in America and nowhere else. One of my very favorite characters in *The Clangers* children's TV show is the Iron Chicken, made of bits of discarded metal.

I like the idea of apps for addictions. Like the dieting app I'm using, something like that would talk to the back of your head. There really should be an app for carbon reduction. We should talk to each other in terms of pleasure and habits, not in terms of good and evil. An app for addiction wouldn't just be a substitute for sitting around in a circle as in Alcoholics Anonymous. It would be better. Those other things talk to the front of your head.

People generally seem to think that cognitive behavioral therapy talks to the back of your head. But when a human being is using it on you, they inevitably get into guilt and religion mode. They start using the front of their head, and your head. "Now that's a bad distorted thought, isn't it? Distorted, not straight. It's queer. You need to replace it with a straight thought. Feelings are distorted thoughts." Guess what, idiot. You just said a feeling, without being in charge of it—talk about distorted thoughts! You expressed a feeling via that concept. That feeling is called fear. CBT is based on fear. CBT is based on a false binary between thoughts and feelings.

I was distressed when the dieting app I used turned on me like this. Up until then it had been a friendly droid version of Jiminy Cricket, only not talking to the conscious mind. More like actual Jesus, who was into wine and picking grapes on the wrong day and hanging out with prostitutes. Droid Jesus drops little hints but never tells you're bad. That was true until I came across the one slogan—the central one unfortunately: *Tame your inner elephant.* That makes a total mockery of the whole thing, and is probably one reason why this app is so popular, because it appeals right in the middle of itself to good versus evil, active versus passive, subject versus object. It appeals to human versus nonhuman. If you change the elephant for horses, you're back in the world of Plato. It's an extra twist that you're in the world of colonialism, the way they say it.

It appeals to master versus slave.

Psychoanalysis talks to the back of your head. Free association, it's not about what you say, it's a lubricant. It's that feeling of letting loose, in your head.

Fuck taming the elephant. Tame the driver. Tame the idea that there should be a driver.

I think my entire career has been about turning into something like an app for dieters, only I'm talking not just to individuals but to groups and collectives and societies and planet-scale, country-scale, city-scale, classroom-scale. The guilt and shame that we manifest at planet-scale. It's terrible. We treat ourselves, as massive groups, in the most childish and simplistic and black-and-white ways. That's what's really wrong with all those big UN and COP statements. They're so incredibly well-meaning. They're so *religious*. No joy. No smile. No humor.

The bigger the group, the more regressed you can get. That's how fascism works. These big childish Live-Aid-style, planet-scale statements are horrible. No wonder the right laughs at them—they have the wrong reason, they're thinking about the content. But the form is exactly as they say, awful, patronizing, condescending, religious, terrible. Those Twitter mobs that can descend on your Tweet like the birds in the Hitchcock film. I hate that. How groups of humans use the front of their brains to activate what Freud called the superego. How they feel all righteous and swirl in ultimate infinite never-ending judgment. How religion is basically that. How at scale, we don't know how to talk to each other nicely at all. Not at all. It's not just groupthink. It's a style of groupthink. It's childish and punitive and terrifying. It won't stop.

Don't punish the chicken. Talk to the chicken.

13

The Stuff of Life

Here we go. Thirteen, unlucky for some. The disciple they don't like to mention. The one whose name is a cipher for Christian antisemitism. The way Christianity is in fact an extra version of Judaism. The extra body in the room. The extra disciple, the "evil" one, the extra body in the room ... and aren't all bodies a bit "extra"?

And what is this "extra"? Why, the biosphere as such.

Ludwig Feuerbach: "*God is love.* Think about it. Flip it around. The verb 'is' implies that you can. *Love is god.* That's how religion works. It flips stuff upside down and kicks it upstairs into heaven where we can't ever really reach it."[1] Reading Feuerbach is how Marx figured out what ideology does.

And love, what is that ... if anything, love is an *affect*. Love is not an idea or an emotion. It's a psycho-physical sensation. I'm going to fix what I've been saying about philosophy now. Neither love nor wisdom are emotions. They're affects. Read on, curious reader.

I think religion is a displaced way of talking about being a lifeform in a biosphere. I think religion is a treasure trove of alienated human superpowers, superpowers like love and compassion and art and spirituality. And I'm far from alone in thinking that these powers come from primates and mammals and reptiles and beetles.

In another sort of book I would prove this to you. But just for now, you're going to have to trust me.

Here's a clue though, a clue that works for me. The "higher" up you go in the Church of England the more sensual and feminine it all gets. The more mystical you get in Islam, the more sensual and feminine it all gets. The more esoteric you get in Buddhism, the more sensual and feminine it all gets. Not disparaging women is one of the main rules of Vajrayana Buddhism, a system in which it isn't true that a nun needs to do ten thousand more lifetimes' work than a monk to become enlightened.

In the background of all that existential stuff about death and understanding you're mortal is an even more amazing thing: birth. You were born. You came out of something else? Out of what? A vagina, perhaps, or a test tube. But whatever in particular you came out of, you came out of a biosphere. I am fully down with Hannah Arendt's and Bracha Ettinger's different formulations of this.

So much philosophy is like so much of "civilization": a massive attempt to block the basic incontestable fact that you are a lifeform.

That's why I'm into religion. Some of it. Some of the time. Science doesn't mean scientism. Science doesn't mean the worlds can be reduced to little bits. Unfortunately, this is the going default PR about science. It spoils the "how" of science, which is about being open and having a sense of wonder and a fearless toleration of fascination and horror and disgust.

Where else to look for the "how" of scientific facts? I think they're hiding in religion, in horribly distorted and violent garb. And I think it's the job of people like me to prise them out of there.

How we look to heaven for all the goodies is how we destroy Earth, where all the goodies are pulsating away in plain sight.

So this is the big reason I study Buddhism, which in general is about pleasure. I was going crazy without it. As a teenage lifeform who enjoys things, but also as a smart, dissociated, really messed up teenager who wasn't told about Thomas Merton and the centering prayer, I was getting another message from Christianity loud and clear: I was the devil. But I was trying to be an angel. When you try too hard, you are a demonic angel. The world is being destroyed in the name of freedom, democracy, justice ... you name it. The world is being destroyed by demonic angels.

I would rather be an angelic demon any day.

Vajrayana Buddhism is all about bliss, aka the back of your head, the "demonic" place—the place that is literally demonic, a messenger from the OOO object part of yourself that you're not in charge of. That bliss is the kind of pleasure that you're not in charge of, that goes on within you and without you. The kind that can even feel a little bit strange or alien or scary. The chicken. Vajrayana talks to the chicken. Vajrayana practices are all about apps. Just say this mantra one hundred thousand times. We won't explain why—just say it and see what happens. Just do this prostration. Just let your mind go, see what happens. It's not talking to the front of your brain at all. It's very very good for the front of your brain, because it's not about concepts. That's been proven, because as I was saying, my meditation teacher's brother, Mingyur Rinpoche, is the reason why we know about neuroplasticity.

Several years ago, psychologists attached electrodes to the head of Mingyur Rinpoche. He meditated (actually, not quite—more on that in a moment). The machinery registered a several-hundred-percent increase in frontal lobe activity. The scientists thought the machine wasn't calibrated right. So they recalibrated it and ran the experiment again. Same result: several hundred percent more frontal lobe activity.

Now they were thinking, maybe the equipment is broken. So they checked it, fixed it, replaced it. Same result. I'm not sure how many times they tried, but it was many times. That's how "they" discovered neuroplasticity. Your brain cells don't just sit there slowly decaying, like "they" had thought. You can improve them. You can refresh them. You can double, triple, quadruple your activity.

And so the disastrously corporate sport of mindfulness was born. What a shame.

The real take-home is that doing literally nothing helps the front of your brain. Mingyur wasn't meditating! He is a practitioner of a kind of Vajrayana called Dzogchen, "the great completion," "the great perfection," something like that. *The great wholeness.* Nothing added, nothing taken away, as a 1980s ad for Shredded Wheat put it. You don't meditate. You "do" a thing called *nondistracted nonmeditation.* You just let it happen, like being on a water slide, or entering a really loud disco, or being on one of those "Drop of Death" things at a fairground. You just "be" your brain.

How do you "do" it? I'm putting "do" in quotation marks because you aren't actually doing a thing. It's hard to describe. It's kind of impossible. You have to hint. But then again, everything is like that, so I believe. OOO says that about pencils. You can't describe them fully. You can only do pencil hints. If you bite one you only get a pencil nibble. There are only nibbles, kisses, licks.

Your mediation teacher points out something incredibly default, called *the nature of mind*. This sounds fancy but it's actually your rat's ass mind, the one you pick your nose with. That's why another lovely tradition, which I like a lot, Mahamudra ("the great seal"), calls it *ordinary mind*. It's default to any thought, emotion, whatever you want to call those things. Any perception. Anything that happens. To that extent, it's like a crystal ball, totally "whole" and "transparent"—words fail me. Everything that happens—that memory, that smell of cake, that pink ribbon on the floor over there, that feeling of dread—everything, anything at all, is like a reflection in that ball.

You're letting your mind be an "object" in the way OOO defines it.

It's not mindfulness. Mindfulness is replacing all the smells and memories and ribbons with one thought, the sense of your "mind" placed "on" something like a breath or a flame or a mantra or whatever. It's like sliding the "OCCUPIED" sign into view when you lock the door in a toilet on a plane. Mindfulness is like the gear lever (or stick shift if you're American) in a car. You don't drive a car simply to show how good you are at using this tool. You drive to get somewhere and look out of the window. Dzogchen and Mahamudra are about driving somewhere and looking out of the window—using an automatic gear, not a stick shift, or better, just freewheeling.

If you read the literature and the media about those electrodes and my meditation teacher's brother, you'll see that Mingyur was "meditating on infinite compassion" or something like that. But he wasn't. He was just being. He was practicing Dzogchen, which you can do sitting on the toilet, having a fight with your partner, screaming with horror, having an orgasm, feeling blank. And sitting on a cushion. You let it happen, then you get all grippy and you lose the knack of it, so you stop. Then you try again. Then you try again. "Short moments, many times." That's why they call it meditation *practice*.

Don't yell. Don't "do" versus "not do." Don't "not do" versus "do." Reality isn't like that. Practice. Hint. Nibble. Kiss. Lick. The stuff of life.

Notes

Chapter 1

1   Denise Ferreira da Silva, *Toward a Global Idea of Race* (Minneapolis: University of Minnesota Press, 2007).

Chapter 2

1   See Timothy Morton and Dominic Boyer, *Hyposubjects: On Becoming-Human* (Ann Arbor: Open Humanities Press, 2021), 61–72; Timothy Morton, *Humankind: Solidarity with Nonhuman People* (London: Verso, 2017), 101–120.

Chapter 5

1   Laurie Anderson, "Born, Never Asked," *Big Science* (Warner Bros., 1982).

2   Khalil Joseph, director, *Until the Quiet Comes*, film for Flying Lotus (What Matter Most, Warp Films, 2013).

3   Micheal Bond, writer Ivor Wood, director, *The Herbs* (Film Fair, 1968).

4   The Wombles, "Remember You're a Womble," *Remember You're a Womble* (CBS, 1974).

5   DJ Shadow, "What Does Your Soul Look Like?", *Endtroducing* (Mo' Wax, 1996).

Chapter 6

1   Rick Strassman, *DMT, the Spirit Molecule: A Doctor's Revolutionary Research into the Biology of Near-Death and Mystical Experiences* (Rochester: Park Street Press, 2000).

2   Samuel Taylor Coleridge, *Coleridge's Poetry and Prose*, ed. Nicholas Halmi, Paul Magnuson and Raimonda Modiano (New York: Norton, 2004).

Chapter 7

1   Doug Liman, director, *The Bourne Identity* (Universal Pictures, 2002).

2   Lewis Carroll, *Alice's Adventures in Wonderland, The Annotated Alice*, ed. and intro. Martin Gardner (New York: Norton, 1999), 124.

3   David L. Bloxam et al., "The Human Endogenous Retrovirus ERV-3 is Upregulated in Differentiating Placental Trophoblast Cells," *Virology* 196 (1993), 905–909.

Chapter 8

1   Jacques Lacan, *Le seminaire, Livre III: Les psychoses* (Paris: Éditions de Seuil, 1981), 48.

Chapter 9

1   Martin Campbell, director, *Casino Royale* (MGM, Columbia, Eon, 2006).

Chapter 10

1   Jacqueline Rose, *The Last Resistance* (London: Verso, 2007), 7.

2   Rob Reiner, director, *This Is Spinal Tap* (Embassy Pictures, 1984).

Chapter 11

1   John Lennon, *Imagine* (Apple, 1971).

2   King Crimson, "Larks' Tongues in Aspic, Part I," *Larks' Tongues in Aspic* (Island, 1974).

3   Fingers Inc. featuring Chuck Roberts, "Can You Feel It (Martin Luther King mix)," *Can You Feel It* (Jack Trax, 1988).

Chapter 12

1   David Eagleman, "Who Is In Control?", *The Brain with David Eagleman* (PBS, 2016).

2   The Doors, "Riders on the Storm," *L.A. Woman* (Elektra, 1971).

3   Martin Heidegger, *What Is a Thing?*, tr. W.B. Barton and Vera Deutsch, analysis by Eugene T. Gendlin (Chicago: Henry Regnery, 1967), 19–20.

4   Timothy Morton and Jennifer Walshe, *Time Time Time* (np).

5   George Orwell, *Nineteen Eighty-Four* (Penguin, 2004).

6   David Lynch, *Twin Peaks*, season one, episode three ("Zen, Or The Skill to Catch a Killer") (Lynch/Frost Productions, 1990).

7   Patton Oswalt, "KFC Famous Bowls," *Werewolves and Lollipops* (Sub Pop Records, 2007).

8   Timothy Morton, *The Poetics of Spice: Romantic Consumerism and the Exotic* (Cambridge: Cambridge University Press, 2000).

Chapter 13

1   For a brilliant explication, see Jeffrey Kripal, *The Serpent's Gift: Gnostic Reflections on the Study of Religion* (Chicago: University of Chicago Press, 2006).

Index